Time

The Ultimate Productivity Bundle - Become Organized, Productive & Get Clear Focus

3-Book Bundle Set

Dane Taylor

not engaging in the rendering of legal, financial, medical or professional advice.

By reading this document, the reader agrees that under no circumstances are we responsible for any losses, direct or indirect, which are incurred as a result of the use of information contained within this document, including, but not limited to, —errors, omissions, or inaccuracies.

Table of Contents

Introduction

Time is something that is distributed to us all equally: 24 hours in a day, 7 days in a week, 12 months in a year, and so forth.

So why then does it seem like some people have so much more time on their hands than others? Yes, everyone has different schedules and different commitments in life – but one thing never changes: we still all share 24 hours in a day. It's my belief that despite our differences in our schedules, we all have the choice to shape and form our schedules to meet our desires, goals, and needs in life. Yes, it may be harder for some than others to manage their busy schedules and actually accomplish everything that needs to get done... but with some hard work, focus, and dedication, I believe ANYONE can eventually learn essential productivity and time management habits to exponentially improve how much they get done every day.

It's really easy to say things like, "I wish I had more time... then I would actually get X done", or "There's never enough time in my day", etc. But when we actually take a look at where we spend our time each day, each hour, each minute... usually we find areas where we CAN make more time. For example: watching 1 hour of TV could be used to prep your meals for the next day, hence giving you more time for tomorrow! So there is always room to take action and make your life more efficient!

In this 3-book bundle set, you'll learn game-changing time management and productivity techniques to help you take control of your schedule, goals, and

success in life. Here's a sneak peek of what you'll learn in each book:

Book 1: *Organize Your Day: 17 Easy Strategies to Manage Your Day, Improve Productivity & Overcome Procrastination*

Learn powerful tactics to organize your schedule, stay productive all day, and make each day as productive as possible!

Book 2: *To-Do List Strategies to Become a Productivity Master and Get Things Done*

Learn how to specifically manage your to-do (task) lists for optimum efficiency!

Book 3: *How to Get Laser-Sharp Focus for Enhanced Productivity & Concentration*

Learn specific ways to improve focus and concentration when working on things so you don't get distracted or procrastinate!

So let's get started!

Book 1

Organize Your Day:

17 Easy Strategies to Manage Your Day, Improve Your Productivity, and Overcome Procrastination!

2nd Edition

Dane Taylor

Introduction

This book contains proven steps and strategies on how to manage your daily schedule more effectively, be more productive, and as a result achieve more in life while also reducing the clutter and stress around you. It will help you achieve the levels of success and happiness in your life that you desire, while overcoming procrastination and disorganization – remember that these are two major things that kill success! It's time to put an end to that now.

The goal of this book is to be a breath of fresh air and also an inspiration for you – if you think that being organized on a daily basis requires lots of time-consuming planning and a strict personality, you're WRONG! It's much easier than that. Anybody CAN take control of their life and organize their day without being a strictly detail-oriented person. The key to getting things done is simply this: building effective daily habits that become a normal, natural routine for you.

This book is going to teach you how to get started doing just that. You see, anybody can just spell out a list of time management techniques that you should follow. But what I've seen in most people is a DISCONNECT between learning the techniques and actually IMPLEMENTING them consistently in their lives. This is where most people fail, so I'm going to teach you how to avoid this and become the most productive version of yourself possible! And of course, there are 17 core productivity and time management techniques you'll learn throughout reading this book. I consider these techniques to be the most essential, game-changing things you can do to improve your organization, productivity, and get things done in life. Without further ado, let's get started. Here's to your success!

Chapter 1: Getting the Right Mindset and Killing the Source of Procrastination!

Before going into all the specific time management techniques to help you become more organized every day, we first need to lay a solid foundation for you to stay motivated *every day* and nip procrastination in the bud. Like I mentioned earlier, you could learn all the time management techniques in the world – but if you struggle with procrastination, it will stop you dead in your tracks. Let's shed some more light on this to help you understand how to overcome procrastination!

What is procrastination, and why is it a problem?

Procrastination is not a problem with time management, nor do procrastinators have issues with planning. They know what they should be doing and when – they just have a problem getting started. Put simply, procrastination is the art of putting off. Procrastinators are not selective – they'll put anything off, whether it's work related, family related or life related. And if you are going to organize your day, you need to find a way to overcome procrastination.

The thing to remember is that procrastinators are made not born, so you can do something about it. It's a learned behavior, and it can be unlearned. In the same way, organization is a learned behavior, so what you need to do is to replace the 'bad' learned behavior – procrastination – with 'good' learned behavior – organization.

If you don't do this, you are storing up future stress for yourself, and this may have negative effects on all aspects of your life – work, family, relationships, and even your health itself. There's an old saying that 'Procrastination is the thief of time,' and if you are a procrastinator, you are stealing time from yourself – time that could be so much more productive if you could only kick the procrastination habit.

Why do I procrastinate?

There are four main reasons for procrastination, and all of them are emotional rather than physical reasons, so once you can identify your own particular reason – or combination of reasons – you're well on the way to dealing with your procrastination problem.

The fear of failure

Some people procrastinate because they fear they will fail, and this is possibly the most understandable of the reasons. The fear of failure can often be pinpointed in the way you approach various tasks and initiatives. If you are one of those people who think about all the potentials for disaster in the undertaking, and imagine all the different things that may go wrong in your enterprises, this is probably you.

You probably don't subscribe to the 'I didn't fail, I just found lots of ways that didn't work' mindset. You probably believe it's better to avoid doing anything that could go wrong. That's going to keep you from success, because pretty much anything that is worth your attention also has the unfortunate potential for disaster. In fact, the more complex and ultimately rewarding the project happens to be, the more openings for error there are likely to be. It's just the way it is.

People who fear failure also tend to worry about their friends and family. They wonder how those closest to them might react to their failure, even if they are usually very supportive. If any of this sounds like you, the fear of failure could be what's causing your procrastination problem.

The fear of succeeding!

Some people are scared of failing, and others are scared of succeeding. That might not sound rational, yet it happens frequently, and the most ambitious people can be affected in this way. There are times when you want to achieve something so much it physically hurts, and when that happens, you will find all sorts of reasons why things won't work out as you want them to.

Perhaps you find yourself believing that, even while you strive to be the best you possibly can at your job, if you are too good, maybe your boss, your colleagues and everyone who knows you is going to expect even more from you, and you won't be able to deliver. Then you could find yourself worrying how on earth you will manage to top your personal best performance, and continue to improve consistently. You may feel there is only so much one person can achieve, but that's just not true. Your fear may be limiting you, but in fact you have the potential to accomplish anything and everything you set out to do. All you need is the right mindset.

Another problem arises when you believe that if you become too successful, even more responsibilities will fall on you. Then your work/life balance could be badly compromised. Maybe you fear success will intrude too deeply into your personal life, and other people will learn more about the real you behind the professional persona. Not everyone is able to cope with that.

You are a perfectionist

There is an old adage that goes like this: 'If a job is worth doing at all, then it's worth doing well.' Like most old sayings, there's more than an element of truth in it. The trouble is, some people take the wisdom behind the saying to another level, and if they don't think they can do it perfectly, they will put off doing it – often indefinitely. That can be a sensible strategy in some ways, since putting a little distance between yourself and a project that's causing you headaches will mean you can return to it later with some fresh ideas and renewed motivation. The problems start when 'later' never comes. That's procrastination, and it's probably because you're a perfectionist. If that's the case, maybe you should learn train yourself to set your expectations of yourself at a more realistic and achievable level.

The response to an authoritarian environment as a child

As has been mentioned, procrastination is learned behavior that is often an instinctive response to early life experiences. You might have been born American, English or whatever, but one thing is certain - you were not born a procrastinator. That came about because at some stage, you rebelled against strictures you could do nothing about. Procrastination is your way of fighting back.

Perhaps your Mom or Dad was strict when you were a kid. You either could not or would not defy them openly, so you became a procrastinator as a kind of defense mechanism. Alongside this, your self-development in the planning and organizing area would have suffered because you grew up in the background of an authoritarian home environment.

When you grow up in a home which is highly regulated and controlled, when you are instructed what to do and when you should do it, you will inevitably miss out on one of life's vital skills. You don't get the chance to learn how to formulate and adhere to schedules, or how to produce a workable 'to do' list to ensure that everything gets done at the right time so the project comes together as it should.

As a result of such a strict upbringing, it's likely that you rely on friends rather than your family for support. The problem is, friends can be so much more tolerant of any shortcomings and accept your excuses more readily. Friends probably do not see your procrastination as a real problem, and this can serve to reinforce and perhaps even validate your problem behavior.

While these root causes may be behind your procrastination, sometimes it's just a question of wanting to do something else

– anything else! – rather than just getting on with what needs to be done. It could be that if your procrastination habits are deeply ingrained, or if you can't identify the root cause, you may need specialist help. However, assuming that you know what's causing the problem, these strategies can help you overcome procrastination and get on with the business of becoming more organized and successful in life.

Make lists

Just about any task you can think of can be converted into a list. And in fact, nothing is more motivational than a list that you can cross things off as you achieve them – provided the list is not so long that it's depressing. Try breaking down various tasks into a number of bite-sized chunks. If you're not sure how to go about this, just think of elements of the task that you can complete in no more than 15 – 30 minutes.

It's preferable for a procrastinator to complete four fifteen minute objectives rather than a single hour-long task. That's because four separate items can be checked off your list, rather than just one. There's a buzz that goes with that achievement which will help to keep you motivated through the remainder of the project.

Talk yourself into it

Don't use words like 'should,' 'must' and 'have to' in conjunction with the project you're putting off. These words have negative connotations. You need to train yourself to think of the task ahead as something you want to do, as opposed to something you have to do.

You must have wanted to undertake the project in the first place, or you wouldn't have committed to it. You need to view the task as something enjoyable that you really want to do, and that means adjusting your internal vocabulary to suit the situation. Choose more positive words to use – convince yourself that you want to do the task, tell yourself you're going to enjoy it – and believe it!

Do something – anything at all!

Often, procrastinators find that getting started on a project is the main problem. If this sounds like you, resolve to do something – anything – to get started on the task. Simply putting a title at the top of a page can be the boost that generates ideas, but even if it doesn't, the title will be fixed in your brain, and that will get you thinking about the task ahead of you. Thinking often leads to action, and before you know it, you're working on the very thing you've been putting off.

If you need to interview specific people for the project, make some calls or send some emails and schedule those interviews. Once they're arranged, you'll need to think about the questions you're going to ask, and the answers you're looking for. That will give your thoughts a specific focus, rather than having them chasing each other around your brain with no real direction.

Visualize the project

Map out the project in your mind, and ask yourself relevant questions. How will you approach each element of the task? What, if any, resources are you going to need? Who do you need to contact for relevant information or advice? Now consider what the finished project will mean to you, and how others may be touched or influenced by it.

Do you need to get important information 'out there?' Is this project going to make life easier for yourself, or for other people? Can you anticipate a period of relaxation when the project is completed? These are all excellent motivators to get working and follow the project through to its conclusion. Visualize the task ahead of you, then go ahead and do it. Now you've played it through in your mind, it's time to put those thoughts into action and get results.

Maybe you have noticed that all the strategies mentioned here are reliant on re-structuring your basic thought patterns, not making adjustments to your schedule. That should convince you that procrastination is a state of mind, not an inability to act. Until you are able to distance yourself from the procrastinating mindset, the success you are aiming for is always going to be something you hope is going to happen 'One Day.' If you are able to overcome procrastination, 'One Day' will arrive much sooner than you ever imagined!

Chapter 2: Identifying Your Why And Overcoming Negativity

The first step to taking control of your life's direction and becoming super productive is to identify a solid Why in your life. Simply put, what is your primary motivator to get out of bed every day and live your life? Having a strong "Why" will keep you motivated every day to take action and stay on top of things. This is because you'll have a goal in sight with a strong reason to achieve it. Your "Why" will be something you can remind yourself of every day when you wake up to motivate yourself and feel like you have purpose.

It's not as simple as it seems, though. You're going to have to dig deep inside yourself and ask yourself a lot of possibly challenging questions in order to identify your particular Why. It's not just a matter of knowing your goals, although that's a great starting point. You also need to understand why those goals are important to you. When you can understand that, you have your Why.

Your Why should be positive and entirely personal, and it should be a long term, sustainable thing that is not dependent on other people or events. While you may want to succeed because you want to give your family the things you missed out on as a child, the motivation to do so must come from yourself, not from someone else. If it is not your Why, it will not work for you. You need to understand that right from the start, because it's important.

Try this exercise to get you thinking about your personal Why. Take out a piece of paper and a pen and write out your primary goals in life right now. Then write out the strongest reasons why you want to achieve those goals. Here is a simple example to get you started):

Goal: I want to build a business on the side that makes me more money and allows me to quit my job.

Why: I want to have more freedom with my time and finances to enjoy life better and spend more time with family.

Keep working on this, and think of as many goals as you can, large and small. Writing them down as opposed to typing them out will help with the thought processes. And keep thinking about the reasoning and motivations behind those goals. Spend as long as you need to on this.

By having some strong reasons like this to motivate you, there will be no stopping you! Once you have your completed list, type it up and print it out, and keep these written statements somewhere you can look over them every morning when you start your day. Identifying your Why is one of the most useful things you can do to set about organizing yourself and becoming more productive. These are some of the reasons why you should identify your Why.

It's a target

To be more organized, you need to be more focused. Identifying your Why forces you to focus on what you want to achieve, and why those achievements are important to you. You now have a reason to get out of bed every day, a reason to keep going when things get tough, a reason to push yourself harder when you feel like giving up, and a reason to feel proud of yourself when things work out the way you want them to.

As you work, you will keep your Why foremost in your mind – it will act as a target towards which you are constantly working, in good times and in bad. It will help you to work harder, work longer, and work more efficiently. When things go wrong – which they inevitably will – remember your Why and keep going. It will all be worth it in the end.

It helps your belief in yourself

People will doubt your ability at times, and you will doubt yourself. It's bound to happen, and there's nothing you can do about it but focus on your Why and believe in yourself and your goals. You can do whatever you want to, because you know exactly why you are doing it. If you need to or want to, you can explain this to others, or you can just hold it in your heart to get you through the doubt.

It helps you to plan and succeed

Knowing exactly why you are doing what you do gives you focus. It helps you to see things more clearly, so that you can work around obstacles, plan for problems, and eventually succeed in business and in life. Without a Why you can waste time, energy, resources and opportunities. To really succeed, your Why should be personal and emotional, because it will have to sustain you through everything you face until you finally find the success you've been working for.

Once you have identified your Why, remember to keep it in the forefront of your mind and your life. Remind yourself of your Why at least once a day, and revisit it in case it needs to change in some way to keep pace with your progress.

Remember your Why isn't about material things – it's about the difference that material things can make to your life when you are successful. Your Why is your reason for getting out of bed, and while you won't get out of bed for a fancy car, you may get out of bed to enjoy the family road trip you can take in that car, and revel in the pleasure of being able to do something good for the people you love, because you identified your Why and kept sight of it all the time.

Overcoming Negativity

Now you've taken the positive step of identifying your Why, you need to be aware of the negative beliefs that are also being held inside you. This is the #1 source of procrastination, and that's basically what procrastination is: putting things off and not taking action because of a fear or negative belief that you can't achieve your goal. It may be that you're afraid of failure, or it could be that you don't believe you are worthy of having success, or it could even be that you just don't know what your "WHY" is (if that's the case, find one!). I'm here to tell you right now that YOU ARE worthy of success and achieving everything you've dreamed of! Don't let anyone tell you otherwise, including yourself.

Take a moment to close your eyes, take a deep breath, and say, "I am completely able to achieve [state your goal here]." Take note of what negative thoughts you feel, if any, when you say this. This will help you identify what negative beliefs about yourself are inside you. Identify them, write them out, and then write out an opposite positive belief that you can replace it with. Write out all of these new positive statements and keep them next to your "reasons why" statements so you can read them over EVERY day and reprogram your thinking. By doing this, you will set the stage for a VERY productive life where nothing can stop you and procrastination will be no more.

Carry this over to every aspect of your thinking. If you think negatively, turn that thought into a positive one. If you can just see you are going to fail, see yourself succeeding instead. Change your vocabulary around and ditch those negative words, because they are holding you back. Don't say 'I can't do this,' say 'I can do this.' Or if you're not quite ready for that yet, say 'I will be able to do this soon.'

Have faith in yourself, and believe that you can succeed, because if you don't believe in yourself, you are setting yourself up for failure. And if you have no faith in your abilities, other people will pick up on that too, and you will find yourself in the middle of a self-fulfilling prophecy. You are your own best advertisement, so cultivate a positive attitude. Straighten up, smile, and look like you can do anything you set your mind to. Now believe your own publicity and get out and do just that!

Take a while to practice your positivity before moving on to the next chapter. Your future self will thank you for it!

Chapter 3: The Importance of Building Routine Habits

Now that we've helped you to get rid of your main sources of procrastination, let's move on to the next part of this quest for productivity, because getting your mindset in the right place is only half the battle. The other side of the productivity coin is all about TAKING ACTION. And the best way to do that is to build solid, regular habits that you can follow and stick to day in and day out. I'm talking about habits that will enable you to stay on top of your goals and to-dos every day, week, and month.

When you have a regular routine in place and protect it conscientiously, you are protecting yourself from all the outside distractions in life that seep in and knock you off course. The great thing about building productive habits is that the more you do them, the more natural they feel and the harder it is to stop doing them! We're all about building GOOD habits here, not bad ones!

Willpower alone is not enough to guarantee success, although to succeed at anything, you need a certain amount of willpower. It's a case of planning for success, and the way to do that is to cultivate good business habits and establish a routine that will keep you going and keep you achieving when willpower is in short supply. Willpower is finite – there will come a time when your supply has dwindled to nothing, and that's when habit will kick in and carry you through.

Throughout the rest of this book I'm going to talk about 17 core habits and techniques (or as I like to call them, "productivity hacks") that you can easily implement in your life to help you complete your daily activities and tasks better, become more successful, or start that new career you've been dreaming of, or even start that business you've always wanted to start. This will show you how to stop saying "I don't have enough time!" and how to make time for yourself! By following these principles you'll also end up feeling a lot less stressed and cluttered. You'll be a productivity powerhouse so that no matter what you have going on in your life, you will be able to get everything done that needs to get done!

So let's jump right in and get started!

Chapter 4: The 17 Habits That Will Enable You To Be Organized And Productive

If you can incorporate these productivity hacks into your day, you will soon become more organized, more productive, and ultimately more successful. We're going to look at these habits in some detail, and give examples and techniques to help you get it right, as well as explaining why you need to cultivate these particular habits. Work through them, but don't try to do everything at once. Rome wasn't built in a day, and if you try to take too much on board in one go, you could end up missing out on something vital to your success. This is a marathon, not a sprint to the finish line, so pace yourself, and be sure you understand why these habits are important, as well as how to incorporate them into your life.

Habit 1: Set SMART Monthly, Weekly and Daily Milestone Goals

In order to have an organized day every day, you actually need to think beyond the remit of the present day's tasks. Like I mentioned earlier, you'll have the most motivation every day when you have a strong long-term goal in place. When you know exactly what you want to achieve by the end of a month, you'll be able to plan out your weekly and daily tasks much more effectively and be prepared for anything that might arise. So every Saturday or Sunday, you need to take a few minutes to sit down and plan out what high-level milestones you want to accomplish in the upcoming month and weeks, then break those down into smaller milestones by the day.

A great way to do this very effectively is to use the SMART goal setting methodology. First rolled out in the early 1980s and modified several times since then, it's a way to focus on your goals so they work for you. It's the most popular goal setting tool used today, and you can make it work for you. Basically, it's an easy framework to follow for setting goals that you can realistically accomplish.

The SMART acronym stands for: Specific; Measureable; Attainable; Realistic; Time-based. There are variations on this theme, but these are the most popular ones, and the ones that have stood the test of time. Here's how to get the SMART goal setting tool working right for you, using each of the elements to make sure your goals are clearly defined.

Specific

When your goals are specific, there's a much greater chance of actually accomplishing it than if they are vague or merely generic. So you if you just say you "want to lose weight", that's a very generic goal. Instead, make it more specific like "I'll work out 3 days a week and eat healthy meals every day to lose weight." That's much more specific.

One way to make sure your goal is specific is to make sure that there are identifiable elements in the goal. Who is doing what? When, and where will it happen? In the example above, I (the who) will work out (what) 3 days a week (when) and eat healthy meals (what) every day (when). All of these are aimed at the end goal, which is to lose weight. This example can be applied to any sort of goal, whether it's related to business or lifestyle.

Measurable

Make sure your goal is measurable, and that you have something concrete to assess your progress with. With the weight loss example, you'd say I want to lose "10 pounds within 1 month". There is a saying that 'If you can't measure it, you can't manage it,' and this is certainly true of goals. You need something tangible with which to quantify your goal, therefore you need a way to manage it.

Attainable

Ask yourself, does this goal feel attainable? If it seems way too far out of reach, then it will actually demotivate you instead of inspiring you. You want to set a healthy attainable level where it's just enough progress to be a "win" for you, while also not too stressful or far out of reach. At the same time, it shouldn't be so easily attainable that success is assured long before the deadline is reached. Losing 20 pounds in one month is a lot easier than losing 30 pounds in one month, and it's still a win. Also, losing 30 pounds in a month is neither practical nor healthy. If the goal compromises your health or safety, or causes too much stress in the achievement, then it is not strictly speaking attainable

Realistic

This is very similar to the previous criterion, basically: is this goal realistic? Is it physically possible for me to lose 10 pounds in one month? Does that fit with my schedule, or do I need to adjust the goal a bit? The goal should stretch your capabilities and inspire you to attain it. However, it should not be so difficult, involved or impractical that you lose your motivation. It's a fine balancing act, and as you become more used to setting goals, you will learn how to tailor them in exactly the right way to suit your personality and your own particular working methods.

Time-based

Your goal should have a specific time frame attached to it. Otherwise, you'll have no real driving force to get it done. Set the time line with a sense of urgency, but make it achievable, so there is no danger of panic setting in. It's counter productive if you are so distracted by the fear of missing your deadline that you cannot concentrate on achieving the goal you've set for yourself.

Again, in the weight loss example you would specify when your goal deadline is to lose 10 pounds: 1 month, 2 months, etc? Then give it a specific date like August 10, September 30, etc. Keep it realistic, but also have a clearly defined time frame to work within.

By setting SMART goals, you'll have clear guidance on what you can achieve. And of course, you don't have to set NEW goals every week. It all depends on what you're trying to achieve in life, your schedule, and how much you want to accomplish each month and week. In the weight loss example, you could make it your goal to lose 10 pounds in 1 month, so every week you could check in on your progress and make it your goal to lose 2 - 3 pounds every week.

You don't need to work through the items in the order they are set down here. If you find it easier to define your measures first, start with that. Many business experts and motivational consultants consider that to be the most important part of the goal setting process, but whatever works best for you is fine. It's not a rigid structure, rather a framework to help you to identify and set clear and achievable goals to help you to organize your day and your life.

Once you've listed out your goals for the month and week, break them down into smaller milestone chunks by day, so you know exactly what needs to get done each day to reach your overall goals. It's no good setting goals if you then forget all about them – you need to revisit them and check on progress at least once a day, or however often you feel you need to.

Habit 2: Rise early, reflect, and review your routine daily

There is a timeless saying that the early bird gets the worm. When it comes to time management and productivity, this is definitely true. The earlier you accomplish your tasks for the day, the earlier you get to relax and have more free time. This technique is all about using your time and energy in the most efficient way possible.

We only have 24 hours in a day, and in that day we only have so much energy. Both the hours in the day and your personal energy levels are finite – you cannot continue to draw on them when there is nothing left. And that could mean the difference between snagging the deal and missing out on the opportunity, just because you hit the snooze button once too often!

The most successful people in the world realize this and have found ways to get the most out of their time and energy every day.

Get up early

"Getting up early," means waking up in the morning with enough time to start your day right and NOT in a frantic, hurried rush to work like most people do. You need to give yourself enough time to start your morning right and prepare for your day.

Make time for some stretching exercises and maybe a little yoga, to wake yourself up thoroughly, stretch out those muscles ready for the day and start the day in a calm frame of mind. Hopefully, you've had a restful night's sleep, and after some stretching and a refreshing shower or bath, you're ready to face the day ahead. This will enable you to be in a positive mindset for the rest of the day.

Practice getting up early

If the mere thought of getting up early gives you sleepless nights, you need to get some practice in! Set yourself a challenge of getting up 15 minutes earlier than usual for a week, and help yourself to achieve that by moving the alarm clock away from the bed so you have to get out of bed to silence it rather than just hitting the snooze button. By the end of the week, you should find it easier to get up, because you're going to be more tired than usual, so you should drop off to sleep more easily. Now set the alarm for 15 minutes earlier, and continue until you are getting up a whole hour earlier than normal.

However, if you're still struggling, stay with the 15 minutes for as long as you need to. This exercise is about disciplining yourself to start the day earlier so you can prepare yourself for it before you start work, and achieve more when you do. It doesn't matter how long it takes you to get into the early rising habit, as long as you get there in the end.

Reflect and meditate

As a part of waking up early, reflecting on your life goals and spending time on your self development is VERY important. When you get up in the morning you should make time to take a look at yourself and reaffirm your self-worth and your beliefs about yourself. This makes a HUGE difference on your attitude for the rest of the day and can start you off in a very empowered state of mind to accomplish a lot.

Use this quiet, personal time to examine your life goals and any affirmation statements that you may have wrote about yourself. Now I'm not going to get all religious on you, but I also believe in God or a "higher power" that created us to succeed and wills good things for us in life. By believing in something as powerful as this or something similar and reminding yourself of it every day, it helps lay a solid foundation for success.

Everyone needs something to have faith in, even if they only have faith in themselves. However, many successful people are also spiritually aware, whether they believe in God or in some other higher power. It seems to follow that when you have something to believe in, you find it easier to believe in yourself and your own abilities.

Do something with the time gained

Once you've established the early rising habit, put it to good use and do something productive with the time gained. It need not be anything work related, but it should be something concrete, other than preparing your mindset for the day ahead and reflecting on what you want to achieve, and the progress of your goals. Give yourself something to look back on at the end of the day, so you can say, 'I wrote that blog post/ read that chapter in the book/ did that research because I was disciplined enough to get up early and get things done.'

Review your tasks for the day

You also want to wake up early so that you have time to review those tasks you actually need to accomplish for the day. This will make sure you don't start off the day in confusion or unclear vision on what needs to be done. You want to have a laser sharp focus on what you're achieving for the day! You can do this every morning by keeping your tasks in a to-do list or a calendar or planner, which we'll cover more in the next sections ahead.

Obviously, things are likely to happen during the day which will interfere with your plans and may even mess up your whole calendar. However, if you are clear in your mind about the day's tasks before you actually commence your working day, disruption can be kept to a minimum. Each day, anticipate something going wrong and make sure that you prioritize the day's tasks into order of importance. Then if there are problems, or if something urgent comes in or someone calls in sick, you've covered the most important stuff. Prepare for the worst and hope for the best – and if you really want to organize your day, start that preparation before the working day begins.

Make time for breakfast

You've heard it all before, but that's because it's worth repeating over and over – breakfast is the most important time of the day. After the long night with no food, when your body has worked to repair and renew cells as you sleep, your body needs nourishment and so do you, if you are going to be as productive as you can.

Trying to put in a full morning's work without eating breakfast is like trying to run a car that has run out of petrol – it isn't going to happen. After being asleep for up to 8 hours, the body's glucose levels are low, and glucose is important for cognitive function. Your brain needs food in the morning, just as the rest of the body does, if you are going to be productive.

Any old glucose will not do though. You could eat a doughnut and it will give you a glucose hit, but in 20 minutes to half an hour, you'll need another one. Or you can eat a bowl of oats or a banana, and that will give you a slow release of glucose over time, to keep your brain fed and your productivity at its peak. A healthy breakfast will also give your metabolism a boost, and that will give you more energy.

So, you need breakfast to boost your brainpower and cognitive function, and to give you the energy to face the day ahead. If you can't face a big breakfast in the morning, just have some fruit, or make yourself a smoothie. A single banana will give your brain the glucose boost it needs and keep up your energy levels until lunchtime. There's certainly food for thought here!

Getting up early, taking the time to revisit your goals and reflect on them, planning the day ahead and eating a healthy breakfast will give you a great start to the day, every day. Being able to take your time to get ready for the working day will help you to be more organized and increase your productivity, so be an early bird and be more successful in your business and in your life.

Habit 3: Prioritize using the 80/20 rule

Have you ever heard of the 80/20 rule? It's a great philosophy to keep in mind on a daily basis and really helps you to get things done! Basically, it is explained like this: 20% of the tasks you do will accomplish 80% of your overall progress. Stated another way: In the midst of all the to-dos you have on your list, there is a chunk of them (20% of them) that carry the most weight in bringing you the most progress forward. Because of this, you'll want focus on those top tasks FIRST as they will catapult you to success quicker than if you focused on the tasks that carry less weight and power to accomplish your goals.

The 80/20 rule is also known as the Pareto Principle, after the Italian economist Vilfredo Pareto. In 1906, he came up with a formula to illustrate how 20% of the population owned 80% of the wealth. In the 1930s and 1940s. Quality controller Joseph Juran discovered that the principle applied to quality, and that 20% of goods caused 80% of problems. He dubbed it 'The vital few, and the trivial many,' and experts in all areas have since discovered that the 80/20 rule works for them too.

So for example, let's say you want to clean your entire house this week. There are many rooms and messes to clean up, so where do you start? Using the 80/20 rule, you'd identify what actions would carry the biggest influence in getting your house clean. So, cleaning up the big mess in the living room where everybody walks and sits would be a much more pivotal accomplishment instead of doing something minutely smaller first, like straightening the pictures on your wall or wiping the windows down. You see what I mean? You focus on the BIG tasks first when you have the most energy at the beginning. You can apply this way of thinking to ANYTHING in life.

Whether it's starting a business, managing projects at work, or prioritizing your daily schedule. By managing your day in this way, you'll always be able to make big leaps forward in your daily progress.

The 80/20 rule works for just about everything, and it works in organization because it helps you to focus your efforts on the vital few – the 20% of your daily tasks that yield 80% of your results. That to-do list you have – 20% of it is going to account for 80% of your productivity or output. To make it easier to understand, assume that you have 15 items on your list. That means that 3 of them are the most important ones, because they will account for 80% of the day's progress.

You should be able to identify those tasks from the list. If you're running a website or a publication, for example, the three things that are likely to get the biggest results for you are writing content, getting advertising and interacting on social media. So those are the things you should concentrate on first. They deserve the most of your time, because they will repay you with the highest rewards, both in income and job satisfaction. If anything has to get left until another day, it shouldn't be one of those main items on the to-do list, because those are the vital few, as opposed to the trivial many.

The vital few are the things that put the most money in the bank account, or bring the most people to your website. Most of the time, you will be easily able to identify these things, or you will experience a 'gut feeling' that guides you. When you can consistently identify the 20%, your productivity and profitability will increase exponentially.

Some of the more minor tasks – the trivial many - can be rolled over so they don't take up so much of your time. Things like emails, for example. Don't keep your personal email account open all the time – log into it at certain designated times during the working day, then read and respond to emails in one session, rather than breaking off from one of your vital few tasks to answer an email that just pinged in. If that happens 10 times a day or more, that's eating into the more productive working time, and it could result in something important going unfinished.

As you become more familiar with the 80/20 rule, you will be able to apply it across the board in your business, and make your day more organized and productive. Concentrate on the vital few services that generate the most interest and income, and leave the rest out of the equation. Identify your vital few skills from all the things you do, and use them more. Ensure that the 20% (or thereabouts) of your customers who account for 80% of the turnover get the most attention, and don't chase after the Customers From Hell who are never satisfied, no matter what you do for them. You'll be surprised by how many times the 80/20 rule will come to your aid, once you admit it into your working life.

Habit 4: Use calendars, checklists, reminders to manage your daily tasks

In the midst of all the daily tasks you need to complete, it's frighteningly easy to lose track of everything you want to accomplish, every working day. This is why it's critical to set up a system for yourself where you can easily visualize and track your progress on a monthly, weekly, and daily basis. This will ensure you don't lose sight of anything, so that nothing falls off your radar.

Luckily, there are a number of tools designed to help you keep track of your activities. You can either buy them, or produce your own, customized calendars, planners and checklists. The choice is entirely yours, but make sure that the organizational tools you choose are right for your business and your working methods.

Calendars

Buy or print out a calendar for the next few months, and enter your high-level goals and deadlines on the relevant days. You can easily just Google "PDF calendar" and find one to print out in a matter of seconds. You can use this calendar to visualize your business roadmap and organize your monthly and weekly tasks. Don't get too detailed with the daily tasks on here, this is more for a high level view of things so you don't get overwhelmed.

You'll also want to add national holidays to the calendar – and international holidays if you work with people in other countries, so you know in advance which days are going to be off the rotation. Some holidays are universally observed, while on others it's business as usual. It helps to know what's coming up over the next few months.

You may want to consider using calendar software such as Office 365 or Google Calendar to keep everything together online, and even set up alerts for appointments and events and deadlines. However, it's still a good idea to have a hard copy version – it's much quicker and easier to scan over a calendar that's actually in your hand, and you're more likely to spot mistakes or discrepancies if you're looking at a printed version. Articles about writing always advise writers to print out their pieces when they get to the editing stage, as it's much easier to pick up on mistakes. The same goes for calendars.

Planners

Planners are more useful for remembering the nitty-gritty, day to day and week to week tasks that need to be done. The great thing with planners is that you can produce as many as you want, without confusing the issue. If you employ people, each person can have their own planner. If you have clients, you can produce a separate planner for each client.

A planner will help you to schedule your working hours so you can get the most productivity from them. While it doesn't need to be cast in stone, planning out your time effectively before you begin your working day will give you an operational framework to work with. Always be realistic over time scales – if you think something will take 30 – 45 minutes, allow one hour, rather than having to play catch up for the rest of the day. Nothing is more demoralizing than spending the working day feeling you are under achieving, when all that really happened was that you were too optimistic with your timings.

So, use a planner, but don't let it be a weapon to beat yourself up with when things don't quite work out the way you expected. It's all good productivity training, which will help you to estimate your timings more accurately in future. With all productivity tools, you need to be positive in your approach to using them. You haven't failed if it takes you 75 minutes to complete a task instead of 60 – you just need to get your timings right. You've learned a lesson, not missed an opportunity.

These days, there are many online planners and apps, many of which can be used on mobile devices. If you're good with technology, and you can make the most of the various functions available to you, this can be a great aid to productivity. However, you need to make sure that you are actually using the planner to help your business rather than just playing around with the toys that come with it, because you can waste a lot of time that way if you're not disciplined.

Checklists and reminders

For a more detailed daily view of things, consider getting a good "to-do" app that lets you make checklists for tasks and sends you reminders on your smart phone when things are due. There are tons of apps out there for this, so take do some research and find one you like. Of course, you can always use the good old fashioned route of using a physical notepad planner, but some people prefer to use apps since they're so much cleaner and easier to use. Apps are also great because they usually have built in reminder features. This is really helpful to remind you when things need to be done in the midst of a busy schedule! Checklists can also help build up momentum and keep up your enthusiasm up, as each time you check off tasks from the list it gives a sense of accomplishment.

If you prefer to do a written checklist without the benefit of an app, it's quite easy to do and it's time well spent since it helps you to focus your mind totally on the task in hand. Another bonus with checklists is that they help you to stay consistent, since you work through the same list every time you do the task. And it's also helpful if you want to delegate a task to someone else, because they can see how you do it and maintain consistency.

To produce an effective checklist, first detail all the jobs you do during your day. It doesn't need to be exhaustive, it's just a starting point. Now separate each task, and produce a checklist for it. For example, if one of your tasks is writing blog posts, you may need to check out the latest news for ideas, or research a topic or check out some facts and figures. Then you'll write the blog, and proofread and edit it. Once that's done, you need to choose appropriate images, before posting to the blog and promoting the post on social media.

This is a fairly simple, straightforward example, but it can be applied to any task, any time, whoever is actioning it. Listing the elements of a familiar task is also a good way to identify where changes can be made for better organization or increased productivity. And a checklist is a good training resource for new employees or existing employees wishing to expand their skills base. There are so many good things about using checklists, you'll wonder why you didn't implement them much sooner!

No matter how familiar you are with your work schedule and the tasks you perform on a regular basis, bear in mind the old saying 'Familiarity breeds contempt.' Simply because things are so familiar, you can get into a situation where inefficient methods creep in and go unnoticed, causing you to lose production and even money if the problem is allowed to continue unchecked. Setting up calendars, planners, checklists and reminder systems is a good way to examine your working methods and reschedule or rearrange tasks and appointments. If you want to be more organized and productive, you need to make full use of these resources, every single day.

Habit 5: Stay focused on one thing at a time – don't multi-task!

Contrary to what you've probably been told, multi-tasking can actually be very dangerous to your productivity. This is because it spreads your attention thin if you're trying to do too many things at once, and because of that no single task actually gets the time it needs to be completed. Whatever task happens to be next on your list, give your FULL attention to it. It gets done quicker and, above all, it gets done. This will help you accomplish things faster, and the more tasks you accomplish, the more empowered and energized you'll feel.

Imagine how much better that feels as opposed to trying to do everything at once and not getting anything done – this would make you feel demotivated and can make you lose belief in your ability to accomplish things! You really don't want that. Stay focused on what you need to do, get it done, and then move on to the next task. You'll accomplish a lot more doing it this way rather than multi-tasking, and these are just some of the reasons why.

Focus shifts from task to task

When you multi-task, you don't give your full attention to one element. You're thinking about what you're doing now, what you've just moved on from, and what you're going to be moving to next. Your brain is trying to be in three different places at once, and none of those places is a safe harbor for full concentration on the task in hand. So elements get overlooked, rushed, or just not completed properly. Or you make a mistake and have to start over. Sometimes it's best to just concentrate on one thing at a time – particularly when it's business related. And the problem is, if you're a habitual multi-tasker, when you do try to focus on one task, you won't be able to, because your brain is programmed to flit between tasks.

More stressful

Multi-tasking causes raised levels of the stress hormone cortisol. While some stress is a good thing, too much can make you more impatient, impulsive and aggressive, raise blood pressure and put you at risk of cardiovascular disease. So, multi-tasking can cause chemical changes in the brain, which in turn can have lasting effects on both your physical and mental health. And that is certainly not conducive to better organization and higher productivity. Multi-tasking literally messes around with your mind!

It's taxing for the brain

Despite common perception, the human brain is not programmed for multi-tasking. Aside from the chemical changes that take place, brain scan research shows that rather than balancing tasks competently, the brain darts between them, so everything suffers. The brain is happiest when it's concentrating on a series of tasks in succession, one after the other, rather than trying to cope with two, three or even more tasks at the same time. And it's worse when you try to do similar tasks at the same time, such as communication-related tasks such as speaking on the phone and responding to an email. These activities use the same section of the brain, and it competes with itself for priority, which means it gets itself in a mess and nothing gets done properly, if at all.

Reduced efficiency

Research has shown that multi-tasking can actually decrease efficiency by as much as 40%. People work faster, but actually accomplish less, because of the distractions caused as a result of multi-tasking. You are more likely to make mistakes, which may result in the need to go back and start the task again. Also, each time you switch tasks, you have to close off one before you start on another, and this all takes valuable time which can be better utilized on other projects.

All the latest business thinking points to the fact that multi-tasking is inefficient and not conducive to better organization and increased productivity. It's much better for your emotional and physical health to concentrate on one task at a time, and complete that before moving on to the next. Save multi-tasking for your leisure hours when productivity doesn't matter, if you really want to try it.

Habit 6: Have an organized place to record your thoughts

As trivial as it may sound, having a way to write things down throughout your day and store your thoughts is a great habit to get into. In life, spur of the moment things always come up, so you have to be ready for that. During your day you may have a new idea, project, or something else come up that you need to write down before you forget about it. This could be for something that needs to be done tomorrow, or next week, etc. What I'm getting at here is that during your day, you're probably pretty busy and so if you don't write these things down when you think of them, you're going to forget about them later. You can look at it as fail-proofing your life! Be ready to adapt to needs as they come up and change course as needed, because it will happen.

So in order to do this effectively, it makes sense to have a notepad planner or some sort of pad or notebook where you can easily jot these things down on the spur of the moment. You could also use a phone app - it's really up to you and what you are most comfortable with. Then at the end of every day, refer back to this list of things you jot down and update your weekly/daily to-do checklist as needed, to incorporate these new things that come up. By making this a regular habit, you'll always be organized and on top of things and prevent your schedule from getting cluttered and overrun by new to-dos in life that come up.

You may even find that these things you write down can have further uses to you, other than organizational ones. For example, if you have a website, these jottings could form the basis of blog posts, or even e-books. Or you may find them useful to incorporate into training materials for your business. At the very least, they will help you with future planning and scheduling, so don't just ditch your notes when you've actioned them. Think ahead of the game, and if they are likely to be useful in future, hang onto them.

It may be a useful exercise at the end of each working week to spend some time going over your notes and even editing them into a permanent document on your computer, so that all the notes that may be useful to you in the future are kept together in one easily accessible space. Sometimes, random, spur of the moment thoughts can be very insightful and rewarding, so don't be in too much of a hurry to get rid of them.

Habit 7: Review progress daily and weekly

In light of all these productivity hacks and techniques we've reviewed so far, this is another essential habit you'll want to form which will help to tie it all together. This is most likely the last thing you'll do at the end of each day, and it will help you prepare for the next working day. Just as it's important to start off your day by reviewing what tasks need to get done, it's also just as important at the end of each day to review what you have accomplished and make the necessary adjustments to tomorrow's schedule.

It could well be that maybe you only were able to accomplish 5 out of the 8 tasks you had on your checklist for the day, and that could be due to all sorts of reasons. Maybe you just gave yourself too much to do that day, or maybe an unexpected new event came up in your day that you had to divert your focus and attention to. Whatever the case, it happens. That's why reviewing your day at the end is so important, for these reasons.

A measure of achievement

You'll be able to gauge how much you can handle and accomplish on a daily basis. Maybe you started out giving yourself too many tasks to do in one day. If that's the case, you'll start noticing that at the end of each day there were a certain number of tasks you didn't complete. Take note if this is happening a lot, and try to work out why it might have happened. This will help you to analyze your productivity and reflect on what's working for you and what isn't.

The important thing is to reflect and identify where you're

hitting roadblocks, and make the necessary changes so that your next day is super productive! Making this a habit will help you grow and become better organized and more productive.

A preparation and planning resource

If there are some tasks that you didn't complete for the day, you'll need to prepare for the next day and make some space for the tasks you didn't finish today. In that case, you'll have to shift everything around. That means going into your checklist, notepad or app and updating the due dates for these tasks you didn't accomplish and moving them to tomorrow's due date instead. Some tasks may need to be moved on another day, or dropped from the immediate schedule altogether.

The point is to have clear action steps for the next day so that when you wake up, you can hit the ground running and know exactly what you need to do. Don't spend valuable production time trying to reschedule tasks that should have been picked up and dealt with in the end of day review.

You should also do this "reflecting" on a weekly basis too – when you're listing out your to-dos for the next week, be aware of what issues you ran into this past week or what things you didn't accomplish, and think about why that happened. Again, by reflecting and identifying where you had difficulties, you can create a better strategy for next time and make sure you're more successful.

When you conduct the weekly review is entirely up to you. You may choose to do it on Friday, at the end of the working week, or on Monday, at the start of the new working week. You could even do it midweek. Whatever suits your schedule and your working methods is the right time for you. Remember this review is not aimed at beating yourself up for lack of progress – it's about identifying where improvements can be made and motivating you to boost productivity and plan more effectively.

Habit 8: Guard your time and stay clear of time wasters!

This may seem obvious, but many people don't even realize how much time they waste doing "useless" things throughout their day. By "useless", I mean doing things that don't move them forward in accomplishing their tasks for the day. This consists of big time wasters like going on social media, watching TV or movies, playing video games or game apps on your phone, or just browsing random things on the internet. Don't get me wrong, these things aren't bad and of course it's good to spend time on relaxing and leisure, but the issue is WHEN you do it. And this is where most people struggle. Some people go straight to social media the minute they wake up, and spend too much time on it throughout the day.

Obviously, this can affect your productivity in several ways. For one, going on social media or doing other mindless things can interfere with your routine habits and disrupt your schedule. If you spend your morning on Facebook instead of planning and reviewing your day, you're already losing the productivity battle. You'll go into your day with a very unclear sense of what needs to be done that day! Secondly, the more time you spend on mindless time consumers, the harder it will be to break the habit of doing it.

Now, I'm not saying going on social media during the day is bad. Instead, you should ONLY do it when it fits around your productivity schedule. If you're in the middle of something important, don't go on social media. If you're taking a 15 minute break and want to clear your head, then it's fine to go on it for a few minutes. But save the bulk of your leisure activities for the end of the day, after you've accomplished all your to-dos for the day. That way you don't have to worry about it and you won't feel guilty about it! Here are some great ways to guard your time.

Turn off the Internet and electronic devices

The best way to stop yourself wasting time on social media and other electronic distractions is to turn them off while you're working. Be firm with yourself, and only turn these devices back on when you have finished what you need to accomplish. If it helps, set yourself a reward scheme as an incentive. After two hours work, you will grant yourself a 10 – 15 minute break when you can check out Facebook, answer some personal emails or text a friend. Or you may decide that when you have written 4 blog posts, you will spend 10 minutes online.

By setting up a reward scheme for electronic distractions, you are boosting productivity in two ways. First of all, you are removing the source of the distraction, then because you are going to reward yourself after a couple of hours work, you're likely to work that much harder and faster. In any event, it's a good idea to take regular breaks after a couple of hours, as your concentration is likely to flag after that time, so it's a great solution.

Turn off business email alerts

It can be very tempting to leave whatever you're doing and attend to business emails when an alert comes in. That means you're going to spend an average of 10 minutes reading and responding to the email, then you've got to return your concentration to the task in hand. So productivity takes a hit. Schedule times to answer your business emails – say at the beginning and end of the morning, and the beginning and end of the afternoon. Then you can give your full attention to them rather than interrupting other tasks at random times to attend to emails.

Focus on what you're doing

Okay, the internet is off, and electronic devices are silenced, but if you're still not focused on the task in hand, your productivity is going to suffer. So remind yourself of what you should be doing, and focus your mind on the task in hand. If you're having a problem getting motivated, try visualizing the task. Map out the stages in your mind, and imagine yourself working through those stages until the task is completed. Now imagine how good you will feel when the task is completed and you can tick it off your list. Visualization is a classic anti-procrastination technique, and it will often help you to get started on the project. Once you've made a start, it's easier to keep going and complete the task ahead of you.

Keep a time log

Often, when you think you are working for an hour, you may only spend about 40 minutes of that hour on productive work. Other things like answering the phone, replying to emails, chatting to colleagues and visiting the bathroom can eat into that work time. Try this experiment for a day, to identify ways to guard your time.

Turn off the Internet and electronic devices

The best way to stop yourself wasting time on social media and other electronic distractions is to turn them off while you're working. Be firm with yourself, and only turn these devices back on when you have finished what you need to accomplish. If it helps, set yourself a reward scheme as an incentive. After two hours work, you will grant yourself a 10 – 15 minute break when you can check out Facebook, answer some personal emails or text a friend. Or you may decide that when you have written 4 blog posts, you will spend 10 minutes online.

By setting up a reward scheme for electronic distractions, you are boosting productivity in two ways. First of all, you are removing the source of the distraction, then because you are going to reward yourself after a couple of hours work, you're likely to work that much harder and faster. In any event, it's a good idea to take regular breaks after a couple of hours, as your concentration is likely to flag after that time, so it's a great solution.

Turn off business email alerts

It can be very tempting to leave whatever you're doing and attend to business emails when an alert comes in. That means you're going to spend an average of 10 minutes reading and responding to the email, then you've got to return your concentration to the task in hand. So productivity takes a hit. Schedule times to answer your business emails – say at the beginning and end of the morning, and the beginning and end of the afternoon. Then you can give your full attention to them rather than interrupting other tasks at random times to attend to emails.

Focus on what you're doing

Okay, the internet is off, and electronic devices are silenced, but if you're still not focused on the task in hand, your productivity is going to suffer. So remind yourself of what you should be doing, and focus your mind on the task in hand. If you're having a problem getting motivated, try visualizing the task. Map out the stages in your mind, and imagine yourself working through those stages until the task is completed. Now imagine how good you will feel when the task is completed and you can tick it off your list. Visualization is a classic anti-procrastination technique, and it will often help you to get started on the project. Once you've made a start, it's easier to keep going and complete the task ahead of you.

Keep a time log

Often, when you think you are working for an hour, you may only spend about 40 minutes of that hour on productive work. Other things like answering the phone, replying to emails, chatting to colleagues and visiting the bathroom can eat into that work time. Try this experiment for a day, to identify where you are wasting time. Have a piece of paper or a document on the computer and list the day in one hour blocks down the left hand side of the page. At the end of each hour, stop what you're doing and look back over the hour. Jot down approximate timings for everything you've done, and then review it.

Are you happy with what you've achieved within the hour, or do you think you could have done better, and produced more? See if you can do better in the next hour, and achieve more. The time log is most effective when it's completed over the space of several days, so don't rush the exercise. Again, remember the time log is not a weapon to beat you with to make you more productive – it's a valuable analysis tool to help you make the best of your time and organize your day more efficiently.

Learn to say no

If you don't feel you need to attend a particular meeting, say so, rather than going along because your boss or a colleague thinks you should. If your time could be spent more productively, say so. You can always send along your contribution with someone else, if you have a relevant point to make. Ask to see the agenda, so you can make an informed decision on whether you need to attend or not.

When you're busy and your colleague wants to chat, tell her you don't have time to stop right now, but you'd love to hear her news at lunchtime, or over a drink after work. Learn to say no, and prioritize your work and yourself. Don't take every phone call – relay messages through other people to save yourself time and distraction. If you're worried that people won't like you if you say no, don't fret – they will respect you for recognizing your responsibilities and knowing your limitations. You are not indispensible – nobody is. The world won't come to a standstill because you refuse to attend a meeting or take a call.

By guarding your time and recognizing how you waste it, you can organize your day much better and boost your productivity. It's not rocket science – minimize distractions, keep yourself focused, answer business emails in blocks rather than randomly and learn to say no to non-urgent tasks and assignments.

Habit 9: Create a reward system for yourself

Encouraging yourself to be more productive *IS* a productive habit. Rewarding yourself for finishing difficult tasks or surviving a hard day without giving up or procrastinating *IS* self-encouragement. It is very important to remember to appreciate your own efforts through rewards, and here's why: this is actually a productivity hack that the most successful and wealthy people do... because it works!

It's a brain hack that actually tricks your brain into wanting to do MORE productive habits because of the rewards to be gained after completing them! Instead of feeling like your tasks are a dreaded responsibility, you'll feel excited to complete them. By doing this, you set yourself up for major success!

It's not all in the mind either – when you do something pleasurable, like rewarding yourself, dopamine is released into the brain, and that stimulates the neural pathways. Your brain effectively becomes a dog who's received a treat for getting his training right – it's anxious to do more to get another reward, and the dopamine hit that comes with it. In fact, over time, the dopamine hit becomes more important than the reward, so the habit of being more productive becomes ingrained, and productivity gets a permanent boost.

So for example, you could reward yourself to a nice tall latte from your local coffee shop every morning as a reward for waking up early, meditating, and reviewing your tasks for the day. Do this every day and it will set up a spiraling cycle of success, where the more you do it, the harder it will be to break the habit. Pick one productive habit that you can reward yourself for every day, and you will soon see that it will become easier and easier!

You could even have a tiered reward system to match the achievements. For mundane achievements, you could have that latte, or buy yourself breakfast. For something a bit more of an achievement, say adopting or sustaining a good habit for a week or a month. That can be something like a special night out at a concert or the movies, or a meal at that fantastic new restaurant you've wanted to try for ages. Finally, for the really big deal that happens once in a while, reward yourself with an equally big treat. Take a weekend away, buy yourself a new set of golf clubs or some expensive new toy. You deserve it!

Most productivity hacks are based on some sort of review and/or reward system, and that's because it works! How are you going to reward yourself next time you snag that big deal?

Habit 10: Learn when to say "No"

Learning when to say "no" to things is probably one of the most valuable lessons you can learn in life. As has been stated before, everyone has just 24 hours in every single day, and there are dozens of different things vying for attention every day of your life. If you said, "yes" to every single thing, nothing valuable or productive would ever get done. You'd be snowed under and demoralized, and you'd spend more time worrying about how you were going to get everything done than actually doing anything!

You need to learn to prioritize things and be careful about what you say "yes" to every day. By learning to say "no" to things that aren't worth your time, you are protecting your success and productivity, and your overall health and happiness.

This can be applied to any aspect in your schedule. As much as your job or occupation is appreciated for its financial benefits, sometimes it is healthy to say no to additional offers if it will cut into your time in an unhealthy way. Time IS money, so you want to protect your time just as much as you would protect your money. If your friend asks you to join a book reading club with them that meets once a week, but you don't have the time for that, it's ok to say no! Learn to protect your time in a healthy way and find the right balance.

Another thing to consider is who you spend your time with. They say you are an average of the 5 people you spend most of your time with. So who are the top 5 people you are around the most? Do they influence you in a positive way or a negative way? Do they instill productive habits in you or destructive habits? Keep this in mind and learn which friends you need to say "no" to.

How to say no graciously

Most people don't say "no" because they think they will offend other people, or they believe their business contacts won't want to deal with them in the future. In truth, how you say no is important, because that could mean the difference between the other person accepting your decision in the spirit it was made, and feeling rejected.

The first thing to remember is that people – especially business people and work colleagues – don't normally ask you to do things on a whim. If they ask you to do something, it's because it needs to be done, and they think you are the best person to do that. That probably makes you feel good, so you also feel bad about refusing the request. However, if you really can't do it, you're going to have to find a nice way to say so.

Don't keep the other person waiting around for an answer – especially if you have made up your mind to say no. That's wasting valuable time when they could be looking for someone else to take on the project. And be sure you explain honestly why you are refusing the request. Whether it's because of other commitments, the anticipated time frame, or you don't feel comfortable with it for some reason, explaining why takes some of the sting out of your answer.

If you can, suggest someone else who may be able to take on the task, or find another way to help them to accomplish their task. Maybe you can delegate a member of your team to help with it. At least if you explain why you can't do it and offer some help in getting the problem sorted, the other person will realize that you are not refusing their request because you are unhelpful.

Once you've made the decision to say no, be resolute. Don't

allow yourself to be talked around, or you will lose the respect of your colleagues, and next time they want someone to do something, they'll come back to you, because they will decide that your no really means yes.

What does saying "yes" mean?

If you have a problem saying "no" because you're a people pleaser, just stop and think what would happen if you said "yes." Because the truth is, when you say yes to someone else, you're actually saying no to yourself or someone you love. Saying yes could mean you miss out on family time, and that can lead to a build up of anger and resentment which will impact on several aspects of your life, both at work and at home. If saying yes is eating into your relaxation time, you could even be putting your health at risk.

Thinking of the possible personal consequences of saying yes when you really should be saying no should help you to get things into perspective. That will make it easier for you to say no, and it will get even easier with practice.

Habit 11: Learn how to delegate tasks

There is a very under-utilized tactic that most people forget about or don't even think about: delegating tasks to others. Actually, most people probably WOULDN'T want to do this at first glance. Especially in America, it's kind of ingrained in our society and culture to do everything yourself. While this is a very ambitious mindset to do everything yourself, it's also very prohibiting to productivity. Here's why it can actually be very helpful to delegate work to others when needed.

Sometimes you just have WAY too much to do in one day, and in some cases you really can't shift your tasks to later due dates. When this happens, it's very easy to become overloaded with everything you have to do... and then you start to get stressed out, and it's a downward spiral from there. Not a good situation to be in. Thankfully, there are millions of other human beings in the world... and I'm sure some of them could help you out.

So for example, if your day is just way too busy and you still have to clean the house because your in-laws are coming over the next day... you should really consider getting someone else to clean it for you! If you have kids, get them to do it! Give them some sort of incentive to help you out. If you don't have kids, then hire someone to do it – I'm sure you could find a pretty cheap local service or even a college kid who wants some extra cash.

If you're at work and your project list is overloaded, consider outsourcing some of your work to contractors or VAs. You can easily do this nowadays by going on freelancing sites such as UpWork. You'll find tons of people who can help carry your load and make your life easier.

Do you see how helpful it can be to get extra help when needed? Don't be afraid to ask, set aside your pride. Of course, do make sure to thank whoever it is that helps you and let them know you appreciate it.

How to delegate successfully

While you may be unwilling to delegate, nobody can do absolutely everything in a successful enterprise, and the time will come when you have to call on help from someone else. When that happens, being able to delegate successfully is important if you want to maintain standards and keep everyone happy.

Make sure whoever is taking on the task has all the information they need to complete the task competently. Explain what they need to know, answer any questions they may have, then trust to their ability and allow them some freedom. Everyone has their own working methods, and, rather than spelling it all out chapter and verse, allow them some leeway to express themselves and demonstrate their own particular expertise. Make sure they know what your expectations are regarding completion of the project, and then leave them to get on with it.

If you can train yourself to delegate successfully, you'll be among the 10% of management who regularly use delegation as a resource for getting things done. It's a valuable skill to learn, and it will help you to be more organized and productive in your working life, as well as freeing up more leisure time for you to enjoy with friends and family. Shouldn't you be delegating more?

Habit 12: Get enough sleep and exercise

Being organized and productive isn't confined to the workplace and to working hours. It starts at home, with getting enough rest and exercise so that you are fit and healthy and ready to face the challenges the day brings. Sleep and exercise help to sharpen up the mind and improve cognitive function so that you can deal with the challenges that arise during a typical working day.

Get enough sleep

While most people today don't go to bed "early", this is something you should try to get into the habit of. The amount of sleep you get is MASSIVELY influential to the amount of energy you'll have for the next day. Sadly, most people get much less sleep than they need. And since you're waking up early in the morning to get a head start on your productive routine, you need to go to bed in time to get sufficient restful sleep.

During sleep time, your body works hard to repair and renew its cells. This is a task that can only be done when you're at rest, because it takes so much energy, and during the day, that energy is taken up with keeping the body functioning healthily and normally. This repair and renewal process also concerns the brain cells. Too little sleep results in impaired memory function and the inability to make rational decisions, and this can affect productivity adversely. If you start the day off drowsy and below par, it's only going to go downhill from there, so make sure you get enough sleep for the sake of your body and your brain.

People who habitually get less than 6 hours of sleep are less productive than those who sleep more, even when they wake up earlier in the morning. Decide what time you're waking up the next morning, and work backwards from there to decide when you need to go to bed. Your body goes through sleep cycles of about 90 minutes, and it's best to wake up at the end of a sleep cycle so you don't feel groggy. So you should either get 6 hours of sleep or 7.5 hours of sleep, depending on what your body can handle. Test it out and see how much sleep your body needs to be at your best the next day.

Power naps

Try to cultivate the habit of taking a short nap at least once a day, if possible. Research shows that naps increase productivity by at least 40% compared to not getting any form of rest in the day. If you want to have optimum energy and enthusiasm to get through each day it's highly advisable to reward yourself a short powernap if possible – about 25 minutes should be enough.

In fact a 20 minute power nap half way through the working day is more beneficial for alertness and productivity than sleeping for an extra 20 minutes in the morning. Taking a power nap helps you to relax and lowers stress levels, so even if you feel a little drowsy for a few minutes after waking, in no time at all you'll be more alert and more productive.

A doze during the day can also improve your memory and make you more receptive to learning new things. According to research, power napping protects the brain from overload by allowing it to rest and process new knowledge before continuing to work. It can also improve cognitive function by as much as 40%, so the case for taking a power nap is pretty overwhelming.

Sleep isn't the whole story though. Exercise is also important, because just as sleep rests and relaxes the brain, exercise can stimulate it in the right way. All parts of the body benefit from exercise, and the brain is no exception. The obvious benefit to the brain is that exercise boosts the circulation, which means that all parts of the body get more blood and oxygen, which means they function more efficiently and stay healthy. So, the lesson would appear to be clear.

Get out there and exercise

When you exercise, even if it's just one time per week, it actually energizes your body and mind. There's something about exercising that has a rejuvenating effect. Many people experience difficulty getting themselves off the couch and going out to the gym or even just outside for a walk or a run. However, every time they actually get up and do something, they feel SO much better afterwards and have renewed energy! If you have trouble getting yourself to exercise, try using the reward system to motivate yourself. Pick a reward – preferably a healthy one - to give yourself every time you complete an exercise session. All in all, if you exercise on a regular basis and incorporate it into your routine, you'll experience more energy, vitality, and productivity in your day.

Ideally, you should aim for a minimum of five 30 minute exercise sessions every week. You don't have to hit the gym if the mere thought of putting on the lycra brings you out in a cold sweat. Do something enjoyable, and do it with someone else, because that way, you're more likely to stick with it. Swimming, walking, cycling and dancing are all sociable, aerobic exercises that you can do with other people, which will motivate you to continue. And the great thing is, none of these exercises requires expensive specialist equipment. The benefits of exercise for mind and body are numerous, so get yourself moving, and boost your productivity at work!

How exercise can make you more productive

Exercise is good for you – everyone knows that. It boosts the metabolism, and helps you to maintain a healthy weight. That means you're less susceptible to lifestyle illnesses such as hypertension, heart disease and diabetes. To be successful in your work you need to be fit and healthy, and exercise can help you to achieve that. Recent research has shown that exercise is good for much more than getting you into shape – it can actually boost productivity levels too.

Boosts brainpower

It's common knowledge that exercise releases 'feel good' hormones to lift your mood, so it's a great help if you're depressed. But scientists now know that exercise has a direct effect on the brain cells. As you get older, the brain has fewer cells, because the body does not generate so many. This is a process known as neurogenesis. The good news is that regular exercise slows down neurogenesis, so as you enter your 50s and 60s, you're likely to have more brain cells than your more sedentary peers. That's going to give you a real edge in the work place, because more brain cells makes for a more efficient brain.

And you don't need to pump the iron in the gym to enjoy this benefit. Moderate exercise such as a brisk lunchtime walk or a refreshing swim will do the trick, as long as you get slightly out of breath. Just 30 minutes of cardio exercise gives the brain a blood and oxygen boost that helps it to perform better. Exercise also releases various chemicals into the brain, such as serotonin, the famous 'feel good' hormone, dopamine, which helps with cognitive function and increases your attention span, and norepinephrine, which also helps you to pay attention, as well as improving motivation and increasing perception.

Exercise also relieves stress and makes you more relaxed, so you are better equipped to cope with problems as they arise. Really, if you want to be more organized and productive, you need to fit some exercise into your day!

Increases energy levels

You might think that fitting exercise into an already crowded schedule would be tiring, but the reverse is actually true. That's because regular exercise stimulates the body to produce more mitochondria. Simply put, that's the stuff in the cells that produces energy, which is why mitochondria is known as the cell's own power plant. This means you have more energy to do what needs doing every day, and your brain also benefits from this increased energy, so it's a win-win situation.

Studies indicate that people who exercise regularly can boost their productivity by as much as 23%, and these benefits spill over and last much longer than the exercise session. That means that when you get home, you'll have more energy for your kids or your significant other, or just to factor in some leisure activities rather than crashing out on the couch as soon as you get through the door.

So, as part of your campaign to be better organized and more productive at work, you need to look closely at how you manage your time outside the office. Make sure you get enough sleep, and make time for exercise, to boost your brainpower and increase your energy levels. As a bonus, you'll be keeping your heart healthy too, so you can hopefully look forward to a long and active retirement when you finally quit working.

Habit 13: Eat energy-giving foods!

'You are what you eat,' or so the saying goes, and you'd be amazed at how much the food you eat influences how you think, how you feel, and how it impacts on your overall health. When you're a busy person with lots to do every day, it's easy to take the easy option and eat out a lot. The problem with this is that usually eating out does not guarantee healthy food in the right quantities to maintain a healthy weight. The same goes for microwave convenience meals. These are usually pretty bad for you, because they are heavily processed, with added fats and sugars to make them look nicer and stay fresh for longer.

What you want is food that will actually nourish and fuel your energy and productivity. What foods might this be then? It's quite simple, actually – just eat natural. We could go into a whole discussion on different diets and their benefits, but for the sake of brevity here, I think the main focus for any diet you follow should be this: Focus on eating foods that naturally grow from the earth, trees, plants and farms. Try to eat as few processed foods as possible. Things like leafy greens, vegetables, fruits, nuts, and naturally raised meats will give you much more energy and sustenance than just eating greasy hamburgers, burritos, and sandwiches every day.

Another point worth remembering is that when you eat natural green foods, they help your body to be more "alkaline". Basically, there are two states your body can sway towards: alkaline and acidic. Research shows that when your body is in a more acidic state, this gives the opportunity for disease and illness to flourish. "Acidic" foods would be things like sugar, beer, beef and bread. The bottom line is that when you're eating foods that promote a more alkaline state, your immune system is stronger, you have more energy, and overall feel really, great. Just go Google "alkaline/acidic food chart" and you'll see what foods you should be eating.

If you make it a point to eat natural, alkaline-promoting foods, you will feel WAY more energetic when because you are eating healthily. It's a night and day difference. It gives you the energy and productivity to live an organized and productive day, every day.

Just about the healthiest diet in the world is the Mediterranean Diet. That's something of a misnomer, because it's not actually a diet, it's a healthy eating plan followed by the people living in the area around the Mediterranean Sea. It's high on fruit, vegetables, fish, whole grains, pulses, dairy and lean poultry, and low on saturated fats, sugars and processed foods. Eat seasonal foods, because not only are they cheaper, they are also higher in natural nutrients.

The Mediterranean Diet is mostly alkaline, and it's high in antioxidants and Omega-3 fatty acids. That means it's heart healthy, and boosts your immune system, which will help you to stay fit and fight off infections. And because fish figures high on the list of regular foods, your brain gets nourished as well as your body.

As has been mentioned before, being more organized and productive extends beyond office hours. Take a close look at your diet, and make sure it is not holding you back from achieving all you are capable of. Some foods – particularly refined carbohydrates such as cakes, cookies and fast foods – actually drain your energy levels and make you sluggish and unresponsive at work. By fixing your diet, you are well on the way to creating the perfect recipe for success!

Habit 14: Plan ahead for meals

Following on from the previous section, if you're going to make it a point to eat healthy for better energy and productivity in your day, then you might also need to plan ahead for your meals. Depending on how busy you are throughout your days, you might not have time to make your own food on lunch break. Or maybe you get home really late and don't have time to cook a wholesome dinner.

If this were the case, I'd highly recommend you do what people are calling "meal prepping". This is where you think ahead for the next few days or week and figure out what you're going to eat, and then prepare the meals for those days as much as you need: be it breakfast, lunch, dinner or just one of those. You can make everything all in one batch on Sunday for example, then just store it in Tupperware containers in the fridge or freezer until needed.

If you don't already have one, invest in a crock pot. Then you can set a nourishing meal to cook slowly while you're at work. As a bonus, it will save on electricity and washing up, and you can use cheaper cuts of meat and poultry due to the extended cooking times. You should also consider investing in a halogen oven. It cooks up to 20% faster, and uses up to 75% less fuel too.

These measures can free up your time immensely during the week, and cut back on the stress of trying to eat healthily while keeping up with a crazy schedule. Try it out and see how you get on. Remember, you are what you eat!

Habit 15: Give yourself time to recharge

This also might seem obvious, but many people are so go-go-go that they forget to stop, take a breather, and recharge their energy by relaxing. This is a good way to reward and encourage yourself after all your hard work. It's also a great way to unwind, clear your mind and get ready to take on future challenges. Figure out what makes you feel refreshed and recharged, and make it a habit to periodically do that. It could be going to the spa and getting a massage, taking a day to do nothing but relax with a good book, going out with friends, or anything else like that.

The important point is to just get out and have some fun, and unwind. Better yet, stay away from technology for a few hours. Leave your phone and your tablet at home, or just switch them off for a few hours. Facebook will still be there when you power up again!

Remember not to neglect your family and close friends because of your busy schedule. Just because you're being productive doesn't mean you should neglect the people in your life that matter to you! Make sure you are giving your loved ones the attention and love they need and deserve from you. Whether it's your boyfriend, girlfriend, spouse, parents, kids, or best friends – don't forget about them and be sure to make time for them. Spending time with loved ones has a recharging effect in itself as well, and it will certainly reduce your stress levels.

By making time for yourself to recharge and time for others, you'll ensure that you don't burn out and that you can start each new day with the organization, productivity, and focus that you need to keep going. Taking a complete break from the work environment to do something you enjoy can actually make you more alert, productive and creative when you get back to business, so don't pass up on the chance to do something for you, rather than your boss or your business.

All work and no play makes Jack a dull boy, and Jill a dull girl, so don't let that happen to you. Managing your time efficiently means making time to unwind as well, so make sure you factor in some 'you' time, however hectic your schedule may be.

Habit 16: Keep your email under control!

Another often overlooked issue that affects your productivity is how often you spend checking, reading and responding to emails. Email has become an integral part life in the 21st century, but just like social media, it has the alarming potential to become a time consumer and a productivity killer as well. Given that almost everybody has a smartphone nowadays, email is even more "in your face" 24/7. Whenever you get a new email – your phone beeps, you look at it, swipe it open, and read whatever it's about. And this happens many times throughout the day.

This becomes problematic when it happens to the point of distracting you from whatever things you're trying to get done for the day. It may seem subtle, but if your phone goes off and you read 5 different emails and reply to them while trying to finish a task, it's quite possible you just wasted 30 minutes of your day right there. So to remedy this, you need to allocate a set time in the day where you review emails and that's it. Preferably this should be at the END of your day after you've accomplished all the important stuff. You can spend 30 minutes, 1 hour, or however long you need at the end of the day to read and reply to all of your emails. Of course, if you need to use email for work then that's an exception – just make sure your work emails are separated from your personal emails so that you don't get distracted while working!

Another thing to mention is that you can set up rules or "filters" in your email account to route different emails to different folders automatically. This will help you avoid inbox clutter so that when you sit down to sift through your emails, you only see the emails from important senders first (the ones you designate). All the other non-important emails can automatically go to folders where you can read them at a later time at your leisure. To learn more how to do this, just Google "email clutter best practices" or something similar.

If you are willing, you to do so, you can cut down on the amount of time you spend checking emails during the day. As an exercise, make a note of how many times you open your phone to check your emails during the day. You'll be both astounded and horrified! This should provide you with the motivation you need to get your emails under control and organize your day more productively.

Habit 17: Keep your home clutter-free

Last on the list of awesome productivity and organization hacks is - keep your home clutter-free! The reason this is important and worthy of inclusion on this list is because outside of being productive and working, you need a place where your mind and your body can relax.

Coming home to a house full of clutter and messes will NOT help ease your mind after a long day of being busy. This can affect your mood when you get home, add more stress, and even cause you to not sleep as well at night. These are all things that affect your productivity for the next day, so that's why it's so important. As has been mentioned several times in this book, being more organized and productive extends beyond the boundaries of the work place – it's a total way of life.

As much as you find it comfortable fiddling with paperwork in bed or leaving dinner plates in the living room, it's best to put things back where they belong. Simply put, clutter-free surroundings result in a clutter-free mind. A clutter-free mind results in a more organized, productive, and successful you.

And really, don't use the excuse of "I'm too tired to clean." All you need to do is just power it out in 15 minutes before bed and clean up the biggest areas that need it, the areas that affect your state of relaxation the most. Use the 80/20 rule, remember? That's not saying you have to keep your house perfectly clean in all corners, but just keep it tidy enough to put things back in their place every night so that it doesn't get out of control!

If you really find it difficult to keep your home clean, tidy and clutter-free, why not use one of your productivity rewards to employ a cleaner, even if it's only one or two days a week? Think of it as an investment in your success, and an exercise in delegation, because if you can remove that stress from your life, you can free that time to use for increased productivity at work or recharging time at home. Don't just dismiss it as an unnecessary extravagance – if it helps you to organize your time better and be more productive, it's worth every penny!

Conclusion

Hopefully this book will help you to come up with better ways to organize your day and give you more insight on how valuable it is to be organized and clutter-free in your life! The bonus is that better organization means better productivity, both at work and at home. If you manage your time more effectively, you'll have more leisure time too, which means you'll be happier and more relaxed, both at home and at work. And that means less stress all around.

As a next step, take action to implement the things you learned in this book. Start with the first few habits mentioned, which may be a bit more difficult to get a grasp on, and work forward from there. Tackle any necessary lifestyle changes once you are comfortable with the productivity hacks, rather than trying to implement everything at once. That will just get confusing.

Check back regularly to be certain you are doing what you need to do to organize your day better and become more productive. And read more extensively on the techniques you've been introduced to in this book. Review and readjust all the time. If a strategy is working, try to take it further; if it's not, try something else.

Remember to reward yourself even for the little wins in your life - you deserve it, and rewards will spur you on to even greater efforts and even more success!

Book 2

Time Management:

*To-Do List Strategies to Become a
Productivity Master and Get Things
Done*

2nd Edition

by Dane Taylor

Introduction

You may already know that to-do lists help you get things done, but did you know that most people who keep to-do lists don't actually accomplish their tasks? Why is that? Well, that's what this book is designed to show you – and if you're reading this book, you're most likely wondering the same thing. I'll tell you right now, the key lies within HOW you are managing your to-do lists. The good news is I'm going to show you how to do it the right way so you can actually get things done. Even better, with the number of apps and technology available in this day and age; your to-do lists can actually be easy to manage! The strategies shown in this book are designed to help you become a time management and productivity master in both your business and personal life.

The systems that I explain within this book include how to segment and structure your to-do lists properly, and show how this can be used to your advantage. My goal is to give you the tools and strategies needed to make sure that all your deadlines are met and goals are completed. It's not enough to use pen and paper any more. Life is too fast for that. However, with most people carrying smart phones or iPads with them each day, these can be used to really make your life easier. You should have the freedom in your life to actually relax, sit down and enjoy your meals, spend time with family or friends, and continue to live your life.

This book makes the whole thing easier and takes you through all the different aspects that you may come across that help you to prioritize your time with the use of apps and reminder systems that really do work. All you need now is to get yourself ready to revolutionize your use of to-do lists – because once you do, you will find that life becomes so much easier and that you can manage to accomplish so much more.

Chapter 1 – How to Make a Good To-Do List

It's relatively easy to make a good to-do list. Anybody who knows how to read and write can do it. Making a good one however is an entirely different thing.

In making your to-do list, it's important to remember why are you doing it. The single best reason to do it is because you want to optimize personal productivity by becoming more efficient in terms of managing your tasks, which requires both focus and organization. By efficiently organizing the things you need to do, you'll be able to focus better on the things that truly matter.

Only tasks

When you list down the items for inclusion in your to-do list, you must know how to tell the difference between tasks, goals and projects. Your to-do lists should only contain tasks and not projects or goals. When you mix together tasks and projects in your to-do lists, you may get confused. By limiting the items to tasks only, you'll be able to better organize and focus only on things that really matter.

Take for example your spouse or any loved one. Say you want to make him or her feel appreciated and loved on their birthday, which is just around the corner. Is that a task or a goal? That's right, it's a goal that you want to achieve. Now, how do you plan to achieve that goal? Maybe you'd like to surprise him or her with a party at home, which is a project. And what are the actionable steps required to complete the project? These would include canvassing for a venue, choosing what foods to serve, cooking the food, printing the invitations, sending the invitations and preparing activities for the party, among other things.

Imagine if you can how it'd look like if you include projects and goals in your to do lists. If you can't, it'd probably look like this:

  -Throw surprise party;

  -Choose food to serve;

  -Make spouse or loved one feel appreciated and loved;

  -Send invitations;

  -Print invitations;

  -Canvass venue; and

  -Prepare activities for the party.

Doesn't it look rather confusing? Further, doesn't it run the risk of doing some things twice? Now that's what I'm talking about.

Smaller tasks

Good to-do lists are those that can be managed well. The best way to make them as such is by breaking down tasks that are complicated and big into much smaller ones. To the extent possible, include only those tasks that can be done in one sitting and by you alone. Let's go back to the surprise party example, shall we?

Let's take the task "prepare activities for the party". You can actually break this down further into even smaller tasks and ask help from other people such as:

-Researching popular party games;

-Buying materials for activities; and

-Facilitate activities.

As you can see, these smaller tasks can be done in one step or by you alone. As such, it makes your to-do list – at least for the surprise party – much simpler and clearer.

Labels

Now that you've broken down your tasks into simplest and most basic level, you must label them as much as possible with the necessary info. It makes your to-do lists even clearer and easier to manage.

Let's refer to the surprise party example again. Let's say you've limited the number of activities you'd like to conduct for the party to just 5. You can label each of those 5 choices with information like "props intensive", "little to no props needed" and "children's games" or "adults' games" so you don't have to look further into their details in order to quickly categorize them and schedule them in the program. It may not seem much but when you're doing a lot of things, even the few seconds saved counts.

Priorities

The final characteristic of good to-do lists is priorities. Each task is different and as such, they're also not equal in importance or urgency. A good way of prioritizing our tasks is by using the late Stephen Covey's quadrants that was popularized in his classic best-selling book How to Win Friends and Influence People. These quadrants are:

-I: Important and urgent tasks;

-II: Important but not urgent tasks;

-III: Un-important but urgent tasks; and

-IV: Un-important and not urgent tasks.

Obviously, top priority should be given to Quadrant I tasks, such as bringing your child to the doctor after having on and off fever for 3 days now and paying your overdue credit card bills. Both tasks aren't just important but need to be acted on now.

Second priority must be reserved for Quadrant II tasks because even if they're not urgent, they're important and neglecting them can have dire consequences. Examples of these would be bringing your car to the shop for periodic maintenance works like tune ups and change oils and regular exercise. Putting them off until they become urgent may already be too late and in these examples, may already cause irreparable damage to your car and health, respectively.

Tasks under Quadrant III should be given very little, if any, priority because while they may be urgent, they're not important. Not accomplishing these tasks only has minor repercussions, if at all. These include tasks like picking up a ringing telephone.

Lastly, no priority should be given to Quadrant IV activities because they're both unimportant and not urgent. Why waste your precious time on them right? Life's too short to waste time and energy on such tasks.

This is a very important aspect of your TDL that you shouldn't take for granted for herein lies the secret to focusing for greater personal efficiency and productivity. By focusing on the big-ticket items first, you accomplish more for the same, if not less, time and other resources.

Chapter 2 – Using Your To-Do List

To-do lists are pretty much like knowledge – if it ain't used, it's useless. Further, if it ain't used well, better not use it at all. So if you want to use your to-do lists well, consider the following useful tips.

Cleanliness is next to usefulness

Clutter is one of the most distracting things in the world, whether it's in terms of physical clutter or mental (to-do list) clutter. Have you ever been in situations wherein you were in a hurry to go but couldn't simply because you can't find your keys? Well, it happened to me ages ago and because of that, I missed a very important event in my friend's life. Why couldn't I find the keys to my car? It was buried in tons of clutter at home.

Clutter can impede your personal productivity in a similar way. When you have too much "task clutter" in your to-do list, it's not impossible that you may actually overlook some high priority tasks as it can get lost in an ocean of other tasks. For the most part, junk or clutter tasks are mostly those found in Quadrant IV, i.e., worthless ones like spending 3 hours on Facebook everyday – unless you're a social media content manager or marketer. One of the best ways to minimize or task clutter is to periodically check your to-do lists to see if by any chance, some worthless Quadrant IV tasks managed to slip in undetected. If so, clean up your list and delete them.

Another source of task clutter is procrastination, which leads to continuous build-up of pending tasks that would've been accomplished and removed from your to-do lists already. These are particularly dangerous to personal productivity simply because they tend to eat time that's meant for other scheduled tasks. We'll deal with overcoming procrastination in more detail towards the end of the book but suffice to say, don't put off for another time what you can do now. Whenever possible, make sure that your daily to-do lists are cleaned up and clutter-free by the time you hit the sack.

Pareto Principle and Parkinson's Law

I guess you're already familiar with the Pareto Principle, which states that on average, 80% of results come from about 20% of resources. On the other hand, you may not have heard of Parkinson's Law up until now. Well, Parkinson's Law in a nutshell is the reason why many people seem to be more effective when cramming – or at least they claim so. It says that a particular task's perceived value or importance increases when the time given to accomplish it shortens. In other words, tasks whose deadlines are fast approaching become more important. I believe the proper term for that is urgent. Parkinson's Law is also referred to the magic of the imminent deadline, according to Tim Ferris in his best-selling book The 4-Hour Workweek.

So why are we even talking about this and what has this to do with using our to-do lists well? We can use the Pareto Principle to determine which tasks to prioritize. What the Pareto Principle is trying to say is that you should give more importance to tasks that account for the biggest share of the results you're looking for. Even without the technicalities of Quadrant logic, you can easily deduce that in most cases, work related tasks should come first. This is why in general, most people spend most of their waking hours on work.

Parkinson's Law on the other hand, can help us become more focused on finishing our tasks and finishing them well. By setting relatively shorter than normal deadlines for certain top-priority tasks, you'll be able to prioritize them accordingly and focus on the essentials. Many times, we tend to complicate many tasks if we're given too much time to finish them. Why?

For one, nature – us included – abhors a vacuum and as such, tends to fill it up. Simply speaking, our tendency as humans is to fill up the time given to us for accomplishing tasks. With more time given to us, we'll probably think of ways to make the task more complicated than it really is. Tim Ferris gave a really good example of this – his own. He said while he was in university, it was already the night before his term paper or thesis was due and still we weren't anywhere near finished. Without the benefit of an extended deadline, he was forced to focus on passing a paper the next day. With less than 24 hours and having to practically start over, he had to focus on the essentials of the paper. By focusing on the essentials, he was able to submit a very well written paper. The lack of time forced him to stick to what's important and that allowed him to do well.

So how do you combine the 2 when it comes to managing your to-do lists? Use the Pareto Principle to identify the important, high priority tasks to focus on and set relatively short deadlines (Parkinson's Law) for accomplishing them. Not only can you finish your tasks ahead of schedule, you can also accomplish them well.

Action steps

When you include outcomes in your to-do lists, you run the risk of either being distracted or overwhelmed that you may fail to accomplish your tasks. Remember clutter? Minimize it by making sure that only action steps are included in the tasks in your to-do lists. No more, no less.

A good example of this is a task that's written down merely as "chest day at the gym". To make it more action oriented, you can re-write this as "Perform 5 sets of 10 reps on the machine chest press using 50 pounds."

And speaking of actionable tasks, starting them with verbs makes them so. Keep in mind that our choice of words can subtly affect how we feel about certain things. By writing down tasks with verbs at the start, we subconsciously tell ourselves that we must act on it. Instead of "blog" for example, you can write the task as "write and post social media marketing blog by 12pm" or instead of "groceries", you can write it down as "get food supplies from the grocery store."

When you begin tasks with verbs instead of nouns, you minimize clutter by keeping your list clear of outcomes as well as making it easy for you to know at first sight what you need to do. Using verbs that can also be used as nouns like "blog" or "deposit" can lead to potential use of outcomes in your task lists.

Why?

If a task has no valid reason for accomplishing, why bother putting it in your to-do list? It'll just be clutter and keep you from doing what really matters and continue being productive. So keep in mind that tasks that to aren't aligned to what's really important to you, impossible to finish or worthless (Quadrant III and IV items), spare yourself the trouble and don't put them on your to-do list.

Time

Each task on your to-do list will require different amounts of time to accomplish. When you factor in the time needed to accomplish them, you'll know if you need to break them down further or simplify them.

One good indicator is that if it takes more than an hour to finish, a task may be too big or complicated. Not scaling back may result in discouragement or procrastination. When you break them down to smaller chunks, you avoid being discouraged or the temptation to procrastinate.

An example of a relatively big or complex task is preparing your home for a birthday party. These may include, among others, house repairs, vacuuming and trimming the lawn. It's a good idea to just break them down into those smaller tasks and treat the original task as a project instead of a task.

If you find that your estimates are a bit off at first, don't despair. It's a skill that needs to be practiced to become good at. You'll eventually get it as you go along so don't be too hard on yourself.

Fast forward

While it is good to focus on the task at hand, good preparations require that you think ahead to prepare for the succeeding actions steps. When you do so, you minimize the amount of time lag from accomplishing a pre-requisite task and succeeding ones because you can immediately hit the ground running on the next one as you've already identified and prepared for it before hand.

Reviews

Reviewing your to-do lists on a regular basis, say weekly, ensures all's in order and help you prepare well for the following week. It shouldn't take more than 20 minutes to do so but the benefits you'll reap from doing so can be so much more. Just like going on an out of town trips, you make regular stops to see if you're headed towards the right direction and if not, adjust accordingly. Often skipping periodic reviews may be an indication that you already have too much on your plate.

Necessary Info

Procrastination becomes even more tempting when you're inconvenienced. Have you ever experienced being inconvenienced simply because you put off things today for tomorrow? Me, I've experienced this before when I kept on putting off doing the groceries simply because I'm "tired". The usual consequence? I end up spending more money for household food by ordering for delivery.

One way to minimize such inconveniences brought about by procrastination is to include important information as you list your tasks in your to-do list. This saves you a whole lot of time spent just looking for them especially when you're in a hurry. An example is looking for a car mechanic to fix your car at home. If you don't list down the contact information of the mechanics you plan to contact as you include the task in your to-do list, then you may spend more time than necessary trying to look for such info later on. If you're in a hurry, those precious minutes can spell the difference between being able to accomplish the task and procrastinate – forever!

Remember, success favors those who do their homework and by including important information or references together with your tasks, you can minimize the risks of procrastinating due to inconvenience.

Chapter 3 – Common Mistakes Made with Time Management and To-do Lists

Did you know that there are wrong ways to use to-do lists? Unless you know how to maximize your use of to-do lists, you may actually be wasting a lot of time. The problems that people have with them come down to a number of factors and this chapter is to help you to touch base on what these mistakes are. You may find that you are using to-do lists but still not achieving and this should tell you what you are doing wrong, and what is getting in the way of your time management progress. So let's jump in and see what these mistakes are.

The number one mistake that people make in this day of mass communication is that people **multi task**. They are so accustomed to flipping from one job to another and if you are one of those who are guilty of this, you need to look deeply into the way that you behave. It could actually be counter-productive. Although people see it as clever that they can multi-task, the problem is that you cannot do many things at the same time and do them properly. There is scientific proof that the brain was made to do one thing properly at a time. Multi-tasking also means that you are likely to miss alerts, or forget them and that you may not be as effective as you wish you were. When scientists did a study on multi-tasking, what they found was that it lowers IQ. The Stanford University study also showed that multi-tasking meant that people were not able to retain information and that's bad news as far as your lists are concerned.

Now don't get me wrong, it's OK to have multiple different tasks on your to-do lists at once, but you should **only focus**

on completing one item at a time. What you need to realize is that multi-tasking is unproductive, and you need to give your highest priority tasks your full attention and switch off all other communications that may be getting in the way of your productivity.

A note on distractions: Multi-tasking also comes into play when you are trying to do a job from your to-do list and are constantly interrupted by phone calls, emails, etc. When you need to concentrate on the tasks at hand, you do need to divert notifications and let the telephone go straight into voicemail to deal with it at a later stage. It's vital that your to-do lists are kept to and that you achieve all that you have on those lists, one at a time.

Mistake number two is a common one: Improper segmentation of to-do lists. By "improper segmentation", I'm talking about the mistake of having ALL your to-dos in ONE list or mixed lists. So for example if you have business-related tasks and personal-related tasks on the same list, that's not good. Everything gets very jumbled together in this scenario and can cause a sense of overwhelming, as you look at a huge long list of everything you have to do in your life, both business and personal. It makes you feel like you don't know where to start or like you'll never get it all done. Besides that, you won't be able to easily prioritize what to work on in the present moment. Work and personal life should also be separated, as this will help you be more present, focus better, and be more productive. So the solution is to keep separate lists for work and personal life, and then one level down you need to categorize your to-dos into different sub-lists based on projects, category, etc. This way everything is organized and you can focus on one to-do list at a time, and you can prioritize these separate lists so you know what to work on and when.

Mistake 3 is including events in to-do lists. You may have events on your to-do list instead of tasks. These should be kept totally separate on a calendar but should not be on your to-do list unless divided up into doable tasks. Remember a to-do list means that only actionable items should be included. Too many people add events and get bogged down by them, instead of splitting these events into actual actionable items that can be crossed off and that lead to the eventual calendar item. For example, if reports need to be gathered ready for the auditors, you do not need to have "Auditor's visit" on your to-do list. However, you need all of the singular items that need to be done in advance of that event on your to-do list with a clear indication of the time scale in which the jobs need to be done.

Mistake #4, which is working without taking breaks, is a killer as far as to-do lists are concerned. When you are productive, then your energy levels are at a high. These times are times you need to maximize and your work to-do list should be gaged so that it takes this time into account. You do need breaks. You need to have a break for lunch and this helps you to be more productive and to restart with fresh ideas in the afternoon. Those whose to-do lists are so long that they are unmanageable are usually those who do not take care of their own wellbeing and who refuse to take breaks. Breaks are not indulgences. They are an essential part of your working day, so be sure to schedule them and keep to them because they help your productivity to increase, rather than taking anything away from your day.

Procrastination is mistake #5 and is one of the worst enemies of people who have to-do lists and the reason that people do this is because there will always be tasks that they do not enjoy doing and leave until the last minute. If you have something on your to-do list that you really do not enjoy doing but know that you must, it's best to tackle this head on first thing in the morning because it sets you up to be productive for the rest of the day. If you get all the jobs out of the way that you really do not enjoy, the rest of the day will seem relatively easy.

Inability to prioritize well – mistake # 6 - is another mistake that people make with lists. It's okay to list a whole load of things that need doing in the next 24 hours, but if you do not prioritize the tasks at hand, how will you know which ones are urgent and which can take a back seat? You need some kind of color coding so that you can see at a glance which tasks are the most important and work your way through those first. Prioritizing is also very good for productivity and helps you to keep to deadlines and get things finished on time. Then they can be crossed off the list. The more high priority items you have, the more you need to break down those tasks into manageable tasks that can be dealt with simply. You may even find that, working as a team, some of these can be offloaded onto other team members if you split it up enough so that people with specialized skills are given the work that they are best at rather than listing them as one item and not really giving any notification on your list of which jobs take priority over others.

Mistake #7 is **putting in too many items** in one's to-do list. Since many people begin their days with many different tasks to finish that normally varies in terms of how much is needed to complete them, prepare for them and their urgency or importance, they often feel tired and demotivated first thing in the morning even before starting their days! The reason? It's not the to-do list per se but the number of items in their to-do lists. This is particularly true for people whose to-do lists are as packed as sardines in a can that they can no longer clear such lists on a daily basis. As they move the unfinished items to the next days' lists, it grows and grows and certainly discourages them.

The best way to avoid this mistake is by limiting the items on your daily to-do list to just 3 important or critical tasks. Since you only have 3 available slots, make each item count. Make sure that these items will give you the most beneficial results and as such, be prioritized over just about all else. It will also help you much if you start with the most important or urgent ones first. By doing it this way, you get to make sure that you are able to achieve optimal results on a daily basis.

Always remember to keep that to-do list in front of you as much as possible to reinforce their importance or urgency in your mind.

It's best to start the day with a particular habit that inspires or drives you to succeed, whether in your career or in your personal life. Doing so allows you to enjoy the benefit of knowing that regardless of what happens throughout the day, you've completed that single most important task.

Personally, the first thing on my daily to-do list is one that's very personal: quiet time for meditation, reflection and prayer. I just can't go through my day without doing it first thing in the morning. I can function well without breakfast, which I try not to skip of course, but not without my early morning quiet time. It gives me the peace and joy I need to get through my days, which are mostly hectic. In turn, it makes me a very productive person.

Lastly, the single biggest reason for many people overpopulating their to-do lists is the fear of leaving out a very important task. While it's a very productive habit to map out the entire week, starting the day with a list that basically incorporates much – if not all – of what you need to do for the week isn't. What it is though, is daunting and discouraging. It also makes prioritizing on a daily basis very difficult. That's why it's very important to map your week ahead and to the extent possible, distribute the most important tasks among the days of the week in a way that there are only 3 major tasks in your daily list each day.

Mistake #8 is lack of detail or ambiguity. Many people tend to not just overpopulate their daily to do lists but do so with tasks that aren't clear, e.g., no definite timelines or measurable results expected. While it's true that being reminded to take action on something important is good, you may only be stressed if you don't know where to start or when to end, among other things.

At work for example, you can write "prepare first draft of report" as one of your tasks in your to-do list. What does that mean, e.g., how many sections does it include, what sections are those and how many words? Preparing a first draft can mean anything from an incomplete one to one that's 50,000 words long. The possibilities are endless – and can be stressful.

Contrast it for example, with a task that says "Finish a 10,000-word first draft of my bank examination report by 3:00 pm, which includes an executive summary, financial analysis for the last 5 years and recommended courses of action on the bank." Now that's clear and detailed. It's easy for you to determine if you've successfully finished the task already.

On a personal note, an ambiguous task could be "tend the garden" while a clearer version of it can be "hire a gardener to cut the lawn and trim the bushes from 8:00 am to 10:00 am." Tending the garden can mean so many different things, e.g., pull out one blade of grass, trim one of the tree branches or sprinkle fertilizer. It's also unclear who'll be responsible for it and when do you need it done. Putting in the details to your to-do list items make them more achievable and workable.

Keep in mind that to make each task item in your to-do list detailed, it should have a particular course of action to be taken, which helps you objectively determine if it was accomplished or not, as well as measurable outcomes, the ability to be accomplished in one sitting or time frame and a very clear ending point.

Mistake #9 that many to-do listers make is **populating their to-do lists with items that aren't relevant to their goals**. Whether at home or at work, irrelevant items tend to produce "task clutter", which can make to-do lists more and more confusing, unmanageable and eventually, discouraging or impractical. Irrelevant task can also make you lazy because if they're not relevant to what's really important to you, there'll be no sense of urgency to do them.

So before you make your list, make sure there's a very good reason for including the tasks that you did in your list. If you include tasks in your list for the simple reason that it's an obligation, think again. Given the limited space in your to-do list as well as your own personal limitations, you'll need to make sure that more than just "required", it's required by your higher order goals and priorities.

If for example, your mom asks you to pick up Aunt Lucy at the airport at 3pm but you have a pending deadline at work by 4pm. If your higher order priority is to provide for your family's needs, you would obviously prioritize your work on a weekday because if you don't, you may get fired. Besides, there are lots of taxis at the airport so you don't have to be there. As such, you need not include fetching Aunt Lucy at the airport by 3pm in your to-do list.

The 10th most common mistake people commit in terms of using their to-do lists is **making much ado about incomplete ones.** Just remember that as much as to-do lists are important, they're not life or death issues. The world's not perfect and neither are you. Just do your best – I mean really do your best – and if you fall short, move on either by rescheduling it or ditching it altogether. Life's too short to worry too much about to-do lists.

The 11th most common to-do list mistake committed by many people is **using such a list simply to feel good about themselves**. How's that, you may ask?

Well, we live in a world where subconsciously, we're programmed to believe that we're only as valuable as we are productive. Further, we've been conditioned to believe that productivity equals being busy. Hence, the busier the better.

And when it comes to busy, what better way to convince one's self than with a to-do list? Many people probably overpopulate their lists to make themselves feel very "productive". And the thing about it is, it's actually very subtle – unconscious even.

I had a friend who once reached a point that he'd want to be a hermit – literally. He felt he had so much "to-dos" in his daily to-do lists that he couldn't finish them consistently, resulting in backlogs that continue to grow like waistlines of many Americans. When I "grilled" him about his plight, it turns out that he was committing several mistakes in his to-do list. One obviously is overpopulating it. Two, he overpopulates it with tasks that aren't really connected to his higher level goals or priorities. Three, he doesn't prioritize tasks accordingly. And lastly, he realized after I barraged him with so many questions like he was in Guantanamo Bay that he felt unproductive and consequently, worthless, as a person if he doesn't have much to do everyday. He grew up in a family where the parents are highly successful but practically non-existent at home because they had so many things to do at work or in business. As such, he was unconsciously programmed to believe that to be successful and to be someone who matters, you need to be very busy and hectic.

Since then, he's ditched the plan to be a hermit. He lives a very happy and content life after working on his need to be so busy all the time. As such, he's actually learned to trim down his to-do lists and became even more productive.

The 12th most common to-do list mistake is including

big projects in the list. By big projects I mean those that entail too many "tasks" to the point it becomes ambiguous and complicated. An example would be my overseas trips.

It used to be that I would put in my task list "go to (insert country name) for annual vacation". More than just being ambiguous and can't be done in one day or sitting, it's also very complicated because going on an overseas vacation involves many tasks to accomplish. Among others, I'll have to determine the best time of the year to book the trip, book the cheapest flight to that country, create an enjoyable itinerary and prepare my budget for such a trip. And even those tasks can be broken down further into smaller tasks that can be accomplished in one sitting or a single day.

These days, I break down such big projects all the way down to the single smallest task possible and schedule each of them in my daily to-do lists across several weeks or months. That way, I don't feel overwhelmed and actually get encouraged as I see how I progress towards the completion of big projects like overseas vacation trips.

The last common to-do list mistake committed by many people is that **they call them "to-do" lists**. I know, sounds funny right? But hear me out first.

The mistake isn't strictly in calling them as such but in the significance of how they treat such lists. Some time-management gurus think that the word "to-do" isn't motivating enough because it's not as action oriented as compared to calling such as "action lists", "commitment items" or other similar names that invoke timely responses. Just don't call them "don't-do-these-and-die!!!" list. That's scary and intimidating. Calling the list "to-do" also isn't "inspirational" according to some experts.

But if you find that you actually take your to-do lists seriously enough and that they actually encourage, inspire or motivate you to get things done, then by all means keep the name. Really, it's all about how the name makes you feel.

Chapter 4 – High Level Goals for To-Do Lists

When making to-do lists, you need to keep sight of one important factor. All of the work that you are doing is leading to something. You need to have a picture in your mind of what your personal goals are so that you know where all the tasks on your to-do list are leading. Having this overall imagine in your mind, you are much more able to prioritize and to get the order of the job worked out perfectly, so that you reach deadlines. Your goal in what you intend to happen at the end of all these tasks. If you have a specific team goal, you need to have all the items on your to-do list working toward that goal.

A good example of this would be work from home people. I have a friend who's a freelance writer who happens to be the head of his household. Unfortunately, he can't rely on his wife nor his mother to help him out with much of the things that need to be done at home. As such, he has so much on his plate.

He uses a to-do list to keep himself sane and productive. But given his limited time and ability to finish everything, he needs to prioritize things on his to-do list. How does he know which to prioritize? By being aware of what his high level goals are. In particular, he knows that his top priority is to provide well for his household and as such, he prioritizes the items on his to do list that are related to or can significantly impact his work as a freelance writer from Monday to Friday. Another top priority for him is to be the best husband he can be and as such, his to-do list on weekends prioritizes items that are related to making his wife feel loved and secure such as spending quality time with her on dates or taking long bike rides with her.

So does this "priority" play out? Well, whenever there's a conflict of interest in his to-do list items on weekdays, it's automatic for him to choose the ones that are related to work. It's easy for him to set aside other items in the list in order to first accomplish things related to his livelihood. On weekends, he puts his work aside – even if there are writing backlogs to finish – just so he can spend quality time with his wife because he knows that his marriage is one of his top priorities. Knowing what his priorities are also helps him to really focus on getting his work done during weekdays to make sure he can prioritize his wife on weekends and vice versa. That's the power of having high-level goals for to-do lists.

Unfortunately, in this day and age of communication, there are many things which cloud your goals or which may get in their way. It isn't going to cut it with management if you tell them that you were unable to finish a goal because you had too many interruptions or because you were overloaded with work and haven't been able to finish it all. The problem is that many people overload themselves with work because they haven't yet learned to delegate or to say "no" and your goals go to hell when you are overloaded because you really cannot see your way forward. You need to make sure that the following do not get in the way of your goals because it's very easy for them to actually hijack your working hours and stop your goals from ever reaching fruition:

IM or Text – If you have this with other members of your team, you need to learn when to switch it off. It can be annoying hearing the ping of the IM when you are trying to concentrate on something important. Thus, you need to switch it off and let other staff members know that you are busy and cannot be interrupted. This applies to text and Facebook messaging too in your personal life.

And speaking of personal life, IM or text messages can really get in the way of your important relationships. How many times have my spouse and I quarreled during our quality time dates simply because one of us would be so engrossed with texting or IM-ing friends or whoever instead of enjoying the moment with each other. In which case, it kept us from successfully accomplishing one of the most important items in our to-do list, which was to spend meaningful time with each other on weekends.

Telephone – Incoming calls can be a real pain because you never know which direction they are going to take you in. What seems like a simple phone call can turn into an hour or so of investigating behind the scenes in order to answer a query. Don't let that get in the way of your goals. If you have an item on your to-do list that you want to do by ten in the morning, switch the phones over to voice mail until you have reached your deadline and only switch them back on again when you know that you have time to deal with those queries. Again, this is reiterating that multi-tasking is counter-productive.

One of my friends, a single mother, is one of the very few superwomen I know. She takes care of so many things at work and when she comes home to her 4-year-old daughter, it's like she just transferred offices. It used to be that people from work would still frequently call her at her mobile number even when she's already home to ask for instructions or guidance on how to handle certain transactions. And that kept her from doing what she needed to do at home – tick off items in her home to-do list.

But all that changed when she decided to turn off her mobile phone while at home so she won't be bothered by things that keep her from accomplishing important home-related items in her to do lists.

Not that she was lazy – she just knew what her high-level goals are when at home with her kid. Because of that knowledge, she's able to prioritize her to-do list items well at home. She also didn't leave her co-workers hanging by shutting off her phone. She made arrangements that make it unnecessary to call her at home such as empowering her subordinates by giving them authority to handle situations that they normally call her at home about. That way, she can afford to turn her phone off while at home and not be negligent at work.

Meetings and conference calls – These can be a nightmare and your department head may insist you take part in these too regularly. If you find that they are getting in the way of ticking items off your to-do list, then try talking to your boss about the amount of time expected for meetings and conference calls and arrange a time later in the day when you are at your less productive stage of the day. That way, you don't waste as much time and still keep the boss happy.

Meetings and conference calls, if managed poorly, can also keep you from accomplishing your personal or home to-do lists. How? Many meetings, to be honest, are unnecessary and they're just too many. Many times, they can keep you from getting home earlier or on time to spend time with your family or finish many of your at home to-do list items like cook dinner for the family, buy your son's school project materials and help him finish it.

I like what Tim Ferris suggests in his best-selling book The 4-Hour Workweek, which is to do your darnest best to discourage such and make sure that you agree to set meetings only when necessary and to keep the agenda short and sweet. That way, you minimize the risk of such things interfering with your accomplishing items in your personal or at home to-do lists.

The goals that you have should be broken down into phases so that each gives you something that you need to do, or that you need others to do. The idea of having a final goal is that you know exactly where you are going and by what time you need to have the job done. It gives you direction, but these goals should not be on the to-do list. Instead these goals should be their own lists. These lists should then be broken down into to-do tasks and prioritized so that you know which order things need doing in and what time limits you have in which to do them, in order to meet the eventual goal.

Note: Procrastination happens when you simply write down the goal and don't analyze it or break down how the goal can be accomplished. You need to draw a chart even if it is on a scrap of paper to work out the priorities and then to work these into your to-do list, making sure that you give yourself adequate time to make sure that each step is covered, the eventual aim being that you meet your deadlines.

Too many people look at the bigger picture without seeing the little pieces that make up that picture and that's a huge mistake. Your overall goal is important but it's not just a goal. It's a series of smaller goals which are manageable and if you work your way toward your final goal, you find yourself much more likely to get it done. That's why to-do lists are important and why prioritization is important. You need to work out a system that works well for you, whether this is a color-based system or a system that uses the numbers of the alphabet to let you know the priority of the job (i.e. A for high priority and F for low priority.)

By clearly identifying your high level goals, it becomes easier for you to categorize and sub-categorize your to-do list items according to among other things time frame, urgency and goals. When you're able to do that, prioritizing certain tasks become much easier and efficient for you whether at work or at home.

Chapter 5 – Apps to Help You Manage Your To-Do Lists

When you get up in the morning, no doubt you look at your do-it lists. You do need to put time aside for mundane tasks such as email and telephone calls, but the first thing that you need to decide upon each morning is what tasks on your do-it list are the top jobs for the day. That gives you a direction in which to work that day and allows you the luxury of seeing how to fit those jobs in with other criteria that may be imposed upon you. How fast you can access the information that you need in order to identify your top jobs for the day depends upon the **type of app that you choose**. Some find that simple to-do apps make this a lot easier. Some are simply set up a little bit like a grocery list, others are more complex. I personally find the simpler ones to be useful, but it depends on how complex your tasks and projects are. Since this book is targeted towards to-do list beginners, I'd recommend you start out with one of the apps mentioned below. They can easily integrate with your smartphone, computer, and tablet.

An app such as **Todoist** is ideal because it allows you to see all of the tasks that you have programmed for the day on one screen and from there to schedule a breakdown of the job and you can also use the app to share with others, which means that you can keep your team informed of what needs to be done. If you are using this app, you will find that it has the capability to set due dates (it's always better to set these a day in advance, so that you know exactly where you are). Your tasks on an app such as this should be prioritized so that you can see instantly which jobs are the vital ones for the day, while the others are lower priority.

Todoist can be broken down into 3 main sections: Filters, Labels and Projects. Each of these has important roles in managing your to-do lists. Projects can be organized in a hierarchal manner up to three levels. For example, classify my tasks as Personal, Family and Work. I'm a bit more particular or strict about work since it's what provides food on the table and roof over our heads, though I'm not particularly lax with the other two.

One of the keys to effectively managing to-do lists is making tasks actionable and simple. For example, instead of putting in "sell my fixie bike", I can put there the different actionable steps needed to actually complete it like "take picture of bike" and "post it online". Because it's much more actionable and specific, I'm less likely to put it off and more likely to act on it quickly.

For every task that needs multiple action steps, I create a project under the relevant category. In the fixie bike example earlier, I create the project under the Personal category, which is very useful when I conduct weekly reviews of my to-do lists because over time, some projects become less relevant. As such, I can easily remove all tasks that have anything to do with such projects.

I use different colors to make each project visibly distinct and easier to track. I can, for example, use light blue for work projects, gray for personal ones and dark blue for family-related ones.

Labels can provide a lot of help in terms of accomplishing tasks in our to-do lists. Personally, I use 3 label types, also with corresponding colors: today (blue), time-based (gray) and items in waiting (green). Items in the today list obviously mean I have to get them done within the day. Items labeled as time-based are those that have deadlines beyond today and items in waiting are those that require other peoples' actions before I can work on them.

You can personalize your own labels. For example, you can use "Church", "Extra-Curriculars" and "Community" as labels, among others. It's up to you. Whatever helps you organize your to-do items better, go for it.

Filter

Filter can help you monitor your to-do list items more efficiently according to certain characteristics. Todoist's filters make use of a nice query language and are very helpful. You can, for example, set up the following filters, with the syntaxes enclosed in parenthesis):

-Today (@today) : These refer to things that need to be accomplished today.

-Waiting for (@waiting_for): Items that you're waiting on others to accomplish first before being able to act on.

-Overdue (overdue): Items whose due dates have already passed.

-Tasks that can be finished in less than 1 hour (<1h).

One of the best ways to manage your to-do lists is by consolidating your different folders or inboxes. With Todoist, it's so easy to add or subtract items to your folders or inboxes for less clutter and better monitoring. One of the ways you can do this using this app is to set up an email address for your inbox or projects, which allows you to add items in your to-do lists via e-mail using any electronic device that is capable of sending emails. Cool huh?

Any.do is another app that you can use and the nice thing about this app is the simplicity. See at a glance exactly what you need to do and although these may not be in depth, they are a starting point that should lead you to a much more complex to do system that breaks the job into smaller parts. With so many apps on the market, you need to look into which one works best for you because every job requirement is different. The main thing is that you are able to see at a glance which to-dos you have to complete and be able to put them onto the app with some kind of distinction between low and high priority, as already discussed.

It's pretty simple to create tasks using Any.do. Just tap the "+" icon located at the rightmost top corner, which is right next to Upcoming, Tomorrow, Today or Someday options. You can input your tasks either by typing them or by recording them by tapping on the microphone icon. As you type in tasks, you'll find that Any.do will automatically suggest words that it predicts you may be typing for faster input. You can also share tasks with other people. Simply tap on the task you want to share, tap the Friend icon and enter their name or email address. It's that simple!

You can make folders for easier management of your to-do lists by tapping the ellipsis located at your screen's lower right-hand corner then tapping on Folder. You can create and label folders for different categories like "home errands", "marriage enhancement" or "business projects". It's pretty easy to add items on your to do lists in any of the folders. All you need to do is swipe down and tap the icon for Microphone, which is located on your screen's upper right-hand corner and speak out the task you want to add. That task will be added instantly in your existing list of things to do. If you want to remove tasks from your folders, simply swipe the screen to the left and then tap "delete".

It's relatively easy to sync your tasks in Any.do so you don't have to worry about losing your to-do lists if anything happens to your device. Simply tap the lower right-hand corner's ellipsis and tap on "Sync" and you're all done. Any.do makes backing up your to-do list data fast and easy.

With ordinary to-do lists, there's the risk of forgetting to do the things written on the list. But with Any.do, that risk is practically null. All you need to do after creating a task is to tap on the app's "Reminder" icon to set the frequency of reminders, location and time.

It's easy to remove tasks that are already accomplished or no longer need to be accomplished. Just tap on any particular task and either swipe sideways or simply shake your tab or smartphone. If you want to do it wholesale, you can tap the lower right hand corner's ellipsis then tap on "Settings", "Preferences" and "Done Tasks", which will list all the tasks you have already completed. You can choose to delete one by one or all in one swoop.

Wunderlist is a great app because what it does is divide tasks into lists and that means you can easily distinguish what tasks belong to which projects or categories. You can also mark certain tasks as high-priority items. I like this for the smoothness of use, it can be simple yet if you need more complexity the app can handle that as well. You can also add notes to specific tasks.

For many years, Wunderlist was so simple that it was basically just one big list of things to do. If you're the type of person who likes a great degree of organization, it wasn't the app for you. But due to insistent market demand, it has added a very useful organizational feature: folders.

Wunderlist's folders are very simple. You can simply drag and drop to-do lists on another list to create a folder that holds them together. While its folders have limited features such as customizable name, lists rearrangement and repositioning in the Home View screen, it's still a very useful productivity feature. Why?

First, it allows you to properly organize your to do lists and their items, which is the very first step in effective to-do list management. Second, you can use its folders to create a list of task you've already accomplished, where you can simply move a finished item from one of your lists to the accomplished tasks folder simply by moving it there. Given that all your previous lists are saved, it's easy to retrieve them in case you need them for reference.

Another reason why it's useful is that you can create different types of to-do lists using the same items and switch between them easily. For example, you initially sorted your tasks by importance then come the following week, you wanted to sort them by due date. Simply drag and drop any of the lists to the other folders and voila, you have updated lists that are sorted out in multiple ways.

Wunderlist is also an excellent alternative for iOS Reminders because of the ease at which you can add new reminders or tasks via dictation. For some, it's even a good enough reason to ditch iOS Reminders entirely.

As an alternative, **PocketLists** is another app which is very good at helping you to recognize priorities as these are color coded and I find that this works very quickly indeed because your mind is drawn to those jobs which are marked with the color red. If you are a color coded type of person, this will probably help you the best to get all those tasks synched with colleagues so that you are all getting things done with the same priorities and that's something that traditional hand written lists would never let you do. The synching on this app is first rate and that means that as long as all team members are on the same kind of system, you can all be working on the same page that is valuable when you have tight deadlines.

Another good to-do list app is **Google Keep**, which runs on Android and is relatively simple. It's fast and flexible and you can download it for free on the Internet. Google Keep can keep text notes, voice notes, pictures and checklists and has the ability to keep your to-do lists synchronized with cloud storage and other devices. It also has reminders that are triggered either by time or location to ensure that you'll remember to act on them and won't make poor memory an excuse. Because you don't need to register for an account, set up categories or import other lists, it's a very convenient app even for first time users.

It's simplicity however, may be considered by others as a

limitation. For one, its simplicity gives it less features than other to-do list apps. Google Keep doesn't have sub-tasks, calendar views recurring tasks or other features to help you plan much larger projects or manage tasks that recur. But for most people, those aren't important because at the end of the day, all they really want is an easy-to-use electronic to-do list. And for such people, Google Keep is for keeps.

HabitRPG is one very unique to-do list app. It's because of all such apps, it's the only one that I know that makes tasks fun by turning your to-do lists into a game (hence the RPG tag) wherein you can level up your characters, trump your enemies and amass rewards and loot – all by accomplishing your tasks! This app is more for those who are into games but would like to use to-do lists as well as it may pale in comparison to other, more popular to-do list apps. It makes finishing tasks a very enjoyable habit.

Remember The Milk (RTM) is web-based time management and to-do list app that lets you create and manage to do lists using practically any electronic computer device even if you're offline. Among other features, RTM lets you create multiple task lists with different filters or fields, postpone or delay tasks and sync with Gmail and MS Outlook.

Again, as an overall habit, it's worthwhile looking at your phone the evening before and prioritizing your work so that all of tomorrow's important tasks are marked so that you know exactly what they are in advance. That makes lists more effective and sharing the information so much easier than in the old days, where meetings or phone calls were needed to find out if everyone was working at the same rate or to the same set of deadlines. That's important when it comes to collaborations and I would suggest any one of these apps, as they can help you to get your to-do list working in the way it was intended, bringing all those high priority tasks to the forefront each evening and prioritize tasks for the next day. Things change each day and this system works well because you can change the priority settings as those changes occur. By using an app like the ones mentioned above, along with the principles shared so far, you will have an effective system to manage your lists and to-dos.

Chapter 6 – How to Capture Ideas on the Go and Incorporate Them into Your To-Do Lists

The trouble with any system is that it is always evolving. Using your to-do app(s) on a day-to-day basis is a really good idea. In order to keep track of new ideas or tasks that come up on the fly, I'd recommend you set up a separate list in your app specifically for quickly entering new ideas/tasks as they come up. It could be called something like "To Be Prioritized", as you can go back to it at the end of each day and assign the tasks to a list and assign priorities as well. A common mistake that people make is adding too much to their actual to-do list, and then avoiding doing it because the list is too complex. So it's better to make note of these things in your separate "holding" list, then review them later and assign a place for them.

The kind of notes that may come up "on the go" are things such as phone calls that you have to make, takeaways from meetings, ideas that may be incorporated into projects that are in progress, or things that people have asked you to do. Thus, when you go to incorporate these things in your to-do lists, the only things that actually get put onto the to-do lists are those things where you literally need to do *something*. Others are dealt with by sending appropriate messages to those concerned to let them know that their involvement is needed, asking them to put this on their to-do list and adding a follow up, so that you can check to see if they have indeed done as requested.

Note: The problem with giving jobs to others is that you need to know that they are being done, so the only thing that needs to be incorporated on your own to-do list is a reminder to check on the progress and these can be done very easily with alerts so that you know what needs to be done and when. The diary on the iPad is capable of dealing with this, so I don't need to transfer too much information and clutter my to-do list. The trick is that when you receive an alert, it is at that moment that you need to add it to the to-do list so that you don't ignore the alert or forget that you had it.

To reemphasize my point made earlier, being organized and doing one thing at a time is vital when you are dealing with technology to keep track of to-dos. If you get sidetracked you can forget important dates and time limits, and not make the correct notes. This can make you look like an idiot when you are supposed to produce work by a set date and haven't done it. When jotting down to-dos on the go and reviewing them later, make sure you always set alerts for the new tasks. Don't just read them, but move them to the proper to-do list or by collaborating with those who have action to take toward the final goal for your project. This helps you to keep on top of whatever is happening at any one given time without going crazy and losing track of to-dos.

The point is that with new technology, it's all too easy to forget things or to be sidetracked and if you put a little time aside twice a day – i.e. in the morning and at lunch, you are able to slot things into your to-do list and then carry on with your day. That's why it's important to have that midday break and it takes seconds to program all this information into your to-do list and then to share with all collaborators so that they know what they are supposed to be doing.

What's so cool about being on top of your tasks is that people see you as having a really good memory when in fact you are **letting technology work for you**. In a matter of seconds, I can answer questions or look up specific information by opening up my to-do lists. That's what I call efficiency and if you can adopt a system such as this, you will find it's a tremendous help to you in keeping yourself and everyone happy. That can be a balancing act at times, but with technology on your side, it's much easier to achieve.

Chapter 7 – When to Work On Routine Tasks (Like Email)

Email is an ongoing thing. The problem with stopping every five minutes to answer email is that the time you use is digging into time that you should be spending on more productive activities. Yes, of course, you do need to answer your email in a fairly timely manner, but you don't need to keep breaking off from your target work on your to-do list to do this. Those that do will find that they really do make a mess of things and are not that productive because they are too easily sidetracked. So you need to set a specified time that you'll check and respond to emails each day.

You need to learn to use your email in the best possible way. If you allot yourself a certain amount of time for email, what you can do is set up an automatic answering system so that people know you'll follow up when you have time. You can change the message regularly and that's pretty easy to do and only takes seconds, but if they get a reply from you, at least they will be happy. The kind of wording I use in mine is standard and I keep a standard Word document with all the wording so I don't have to type it out each time:

Thank you for your email. Please note I am currently busy at this time, but I will get back to you very soon.

That's a standard one, but you can add to it or make it more specific if you have a set time of day that you answer your emails:

Thank you for your email. I check my emails daily around 10 a.m. and I will be replying to your email then. If, in the meantime, this is something of an urgent nature, you can of course contact me through my mobile number.

The idea of these notes is to make sure that your clients know that their email has been received. Then, you need to decide how to fit time into your day to deal with emails without distraction so that you can get through them quickly and empty the inbox. Remember that multi-tasking is not going to help you when you have jobs to do. Thus, put aside half an hour twice a day for emails. This could be first thing in the morning when you arrive at the office and when you come back from lunch.

Then go through the email and browse at each to see the level of urgency of the email. Some will be things that you can answer relatively quickly without too much thought and that will whittle the amount of emails that you have down, once you have dealt with these. Then deal with those for which you have answers and can deal with without having to leave your desk to get more information. Lastly, deal with the lengthy emails or the emails that may require you to do a little more scouting around before you can answer them. You do need to make sure that your filing system for emails is a good one, so that you have information at the tips of your fingers. It's no good going through 5000 emails trying to find that one that gives you the information that you need. If you sort them into separate boxes, you will know where to find them and that saves you oodles of time.

To save you a lot of time, there are certain things that you can do. For example, the greeting at the top of the email is almost standard. If you keep note of the kind of things that you say, you can have one file with standard email templates and if you have an email system such as CRM, you are able to put the template in when you reply to the email. If you don't have a CRM then you can keep a separate file with all of this information but do make sure that you set up your email so that your professional signature is already in it because this will save you a lot of time too.

Routine bulk shouldn't take you that long if you get yourself organized. In business, if you don't know the answer to someone's problem, don't waste time writing back to them and saying:

I am not sure. I will have to check into it and get back to you.

It's not the most professional of answers. It's far better that you refer to a colleague who can answer their query and write back to the client as follows:

*Your email has been passed to my colleague, ...
............, who will be able to get back to you very soon. For your information, his email address is ....*

By doing this, you are taking this off your to-do list, or in fact it is never going to hit your to-do list. Your colleague can take over and your job is finished on this item, leaving nothing outstanding.

That's a much more sensible way of dealing with email and it means that you have not wasted time on things that you don't know the answers to. The amount of time that is wasted scouting around for answers is an awful lot. Once you sit down to answer your emails, answer them. Do not talk on IM. Don't put any of them off until later as later doesn't always come and set up your automatic replies so that they will last until such time as you are back in your seat answering email again.

This gives you much peace of mind because you know that you have dealt with everything that has come in and that all of those who write to you following that session will have a reply even if just tells them to wait. It's better than no acknowledgement at all and it keeps everyone happy.

Other routine tasks

Email will not be the only routine task that you have to deal with and if you can sort your post into priority piles this helps as well. When you are dealing with paperwork, it's best to have a pile that is easily dealt with, that which requires input from others and that which is urgent. Deal with the urgent stuff first thing in the morning and then if you have time to spare after your emails are done, plow into the pile of stuff that is easy to deal with because you can make your pile much more manageable. If there are items of paperwork or posts that need other input from others, then use your camera on your phone and send it to them. That takes seconds. You can also mark it to say that you did that and follow up later on. That way, all you are left with is the stuff that really does need your attention that is fairly easy to get through when you are energized. Thus, after a break or after your meal is the ideal time. By the end of the day, your paperwork and your emails should all have been dealt with, so that you have a clear desk ready for the morning, and anything which was not dealt with needs to be put on your calendar with an alert so that you can integrate it into your to-do list for the following day.

Chapter 8 – Reviewing Progress on Your To-Dos

It's important to have a regular, routine time to check in on your to-do lists and make sure everything is on track. Simply make a calendar event with a reminder to check in weekly on your lists. All you need to do is set aside about 30 minutes once a week.

If your projects will involve others, Google Documents makes a wonderful place to keep all the job details and a place to include all collaborators on a particular job. You need to set for yourself an alarm once a week to review your to-do lists, and this should also trigger several other things:

- Emails to other people involved
- Progress reports from everyone involved
- Problem solving or reprioritizing tasks

It's a good idea to use Google documents for all kinds of things. If you use spreadsheets for all members of the team to fill in their progress on jobs that have been given to them, the columns that will be important will be the date the job was given to the individual, the time limit or deadline of that job and details of the job they were asked to do. There should be a column so that all collaborators can sign off on the part of the job that they have done, giving the date that it was finished and any notes that they feel are relevant to the task. If there are documents involved or you have asked them to write anything up, then these can be passed in to you via Google Docs and you can quickly check it.

Google docs is a great place for confidentiality and each collaborator can have their own file so that no one else can see what they are up to. Once the work has been sent over to you, you are able to peruse this from Google documents and if you are not happy, send it back with a note of what further information needs to be added to their report to make it satisfactory for your purpose.

The same goes for input of sales figures or targets, and you can have sheets that show what the target is and have your employees fill out their figures with details, so that you know that everything is on track.

The best thing about Google docs is that you can get an app and can access this in a question of seconds on your tablet, from where you can immediately alert someone if they have not come up with the goods on time. I find this a really effective way of making sure that I meet deadlines and of reviewing the situation on a three daily basis, although you must set up your own alerts to suit your job.

The reason that this works is that you don't need to bother people when they are working and can see at a glance if someone is late with an assignment that you have given them. You can even use highlight colors to let each member of the team know how much of a priority the job is that they have been given, and also to note when someone is late keeping their deadline.

If you have managerial experience, you will know that you

need all this information days before you have a report to compile and will set dates which are in advance, so that you don't have any last minute chasing up to do. Using your to-do apps and email, you can make sure that people are aware of their deadlines. You can also see if people have problems and encourage them to leave you notes on their progress so that you are always aware of what is going on in regards to the project being finished.

There are some that use complex apps to do all of this, but I would try to use a simple app. I find that keeping it simple actually works better because you don't need to spend so much time figuring out how complex apps work. So using an app like Wunderlist or Todoist is great because they can handle a lot of tasks, while still being fairly simple to use.

Chapter 9 – What to Do When You Start Feeling Overwhelmed

The first thing that you need to appreciate is that everyone feels overwhelmed at some time in their career and home life. Organization helps you to feel this less, but you may still get times when you really don't know how you are going to manage everything that you have to do. There are important points that you need to remember which you may not see as work related, although they will relate to your performance in work and at home. Make sure that you follow the advice given below because it's vital. Here are some tactics that you can use to make yourself feel less overwhelmed:

- Get a decent night's sleep every night
- Try to switch off from work once you have lined up your work for tomorrow
- Switch off your cell phone after hours
- Learn to delegate
- Make sure you are having adequate breaks

The tendency of people who are overwhelmed is to over-do it even more because they are worried about keeping up with work and home commitments. However, if you follow the four pieces of advice given above, you are putting yourself in good stead and the rest is easy. Let's go into some of things that you may find difficult:

Your workload is too heavy – If you have too much work, and you are a little bit of a perfectionist, chances are that you do too much of the work yourself. Learn to delegate and involve other people, both on the work and home front because when you learn to trust others, you can share that workload and still achieve the same amount. The way to do this with work is to assign part of the load to people you believe capable of doing that work and making sure that you include a diary reminder so that you can check that it's being done. Look on your to-do list and work out how much of it you can delegate so that your list is more manageable. Then, make sure that each task on the list is adequately broken into small parts. Often you can delegate parts of the job to others and then do a report on the whole job when everyone has done their part of it. The weight doesn't have to fall completely on your shoulders and if you split the job into manageable parts, you actually take better control of it because it's easier to complete small tasks than trying to fulfill a whole huge task on your own.

At home, be honest with your partner about the amount of work that you have and enlist your partner's help in doing the mundane time consuming things that are getting you down. In a partnership, you really can take on more together and if you are honest about feeling overwhelmed, your partner will be glad to step in occasionally to help you with all of those commitments.

Assess your job - Everyone needs to do this from time to time and if you know better ways that more can be done, don't be afraid to have a meeting with your boss to discuss this. There may be some company policies that are getting you down. There may, for instance, be too many meetings eating into your productive time. If your boss can scale these down to only the necessary ones, that will give you more time to do all the things on your to-do list in a timely fashion. If you find that you are being laden with more work than you originally did, it's actually a compliment because it shows that your boss trusts you, but you do need to tell him/her if you need more team members or more expertise in fields that are taking up too much of your time.

Assess your workload - At times when you are overwhelmed sit back and examine all the things on the to-do list. Don't worry about them. Simply work out the priorities as some will have less priority than others. The problem is that people who do get overwhelmed tend to see the whole list and panic. Breathe deeply and look realistically at the list and change the priorities, getting those jobs out the way that you can, so as to make your list more manageable. Look for jobs that you can delegate easily and move these. They can be dealt with, with the same level of urgency, but they don't necessarily need to be dealt with by you. Look at things that can wait until tomorrow and take these off the to-do list for today, as the sheer fact that the list is too long is what is worrying you. Make sure you mark them onto tomorrow's list.

What you need to be sure of is that you are not being overwhelmed by overthinking things. Often people spend more time worrying than actually being productive. If you can examine your list, decide upon your priorities and delegate where possible, your list will become smaller and more manageable. Then you will be able to attack it with more confidence that you can finish it. If you have never tried it, take a break and do not take your phone with you. Think of nothing that is remotely associated with work and remember that a break should be just that – a break away from everything. The reason this becomes so important is that you manage to go back to your work with a fresh outlook and less procrastination. That little break, whether for a coffee or for lunch, helps your mind to rest so that when you do go back to the tasks at hand, you do so with a mind that is capable of taking on the workload with less worry. Worry leads to procrastination and procrastination leads to under-achievement. Thus, avoid it. Take a break and go back into your work full swing.

Chapter 10 – Overcoming Procrastination

There's nothing more potent than procrastination when it comes to rendering even the most well-prepared to-do lists. Procrastination, the habit of delaying working on tasks until the very last second, keeps people from finishing them within the allotted time period and at some point, can make people feel greatly overwhelmed.

Many different things trigger procrastination in different people. For some, it's feeling so overwhelmed with so many things to do and procrastination gives them the opportunity to "get away" from everything, albeit temporarily. For most people though, it's laziness. Here are several of the most common reasons why people procrastinate. These may be your reasons too and if they are, included are ways on how to address them.

Stress

Stress can be a very big personal efficiency and productivity obstacle. Many people procrastinate because it functions more like a coping mechanism that helps them deal with high levels of stress. The good news is that it is very much possible to manage and reduce stress levels, though it requires consistency and some time.

If you're often stressed and tend to cope by procrastinating, one of the best ways to manage and reduce stress is to simply take regular times out to have fun. To the extent possible, play more and work less. Otherwise, maybe it's time to either find a new job or move to a less stressful neighborhood.

Consider doing something that you would do even if you didn't get paid. Those are the things that make you feel joyful and alive, which are very beneficial when it comes to managing and reducing overall stress. If you love writing, consider blogging regularly on BlogSpot or Wordpress as a form of stress relief. Do you love to bike? Well, hop on yours and go around the block, neighborhood or even the city more often on 2 wheels! Do you love composing songs and music? Why not take the time to regularly put to record all those ideas that are humming in your mind? The possibilities are endless and these can do wonders for you when it comes to effectively managing your stress levels instead of procrastinating on your to-do lists to cope.

Perfectionism

One surefire way to stress yourself out – and procrastinate – is by being a perfectionist and not settling for anything less. Why? Can you imagine how stressful it is to get everything done perfectly? Considering nobody's perfect, we'll never get everything done perfectly. By being a perfectionist, we'll be stuck with the things we can't do perfectly at the expense of other important and pending tasks. It'll just make you want to avoid working on the other task lists and hence, procrastinate. You may also procrastinate in order to cope with stress.

Another reason why perfectionism can lead to procrastination is that if you're given tasks with open-ended deadlines, you'll take forever to finish them. As such, you may unintentionally delay working on the other tasks because of the need to perfect the current one. While excellence is very much possible and encouraged, perfectionism is impossible and discouraged for the simple reason it leads to procrastination and lower productivity.

The solution to perfectionism is simple. Just give yourself permission to make mistakes and deal with the fact that though you may – or maybe not – worship a God, you're not one. You're just human. Another way to convince yourself to ditch perfectionism is this: an imperfectly completed task is much more valuable than a perfectly incomplete one. As the saying goes, a bird in the hand is better than one in the bush.

Lack of skills

If you're not adequately skilled enough in whatever task you need to accomplish, personal or at work, procrastination is a very enticing option to avoid embarrassment. Why? Let's face it, it's less painful on the ego to be criticized as late or lazy rather than incompetent.

By taking only on tasks that you honestly know for a fact that you're capable of handling or by thinking long and hard about taking on tasks that aren't up your alley, you minimize the risk of being in a difficult situation wherein you can't satisfactorily complete a task. And the less such situations manifest, the less incentives there are for procrastinating.

Lack of motivation

Every now and then, we all feel lazy...and that's normal. But if that feeling becomes chronic and persistent, it can cause us to become habitual procrastinators.

One of the best ways to become motivated and get out of that rut is to do a bit of soul searching and determine what your life purpose is (higher order goals and priorities, anyone?). Failure to do so may keep you from becoming the best person you can be and as such, keep you feeling chronically lazy and unmotivated.

Centering tasks around higher order goals and priorities can help significantly reduce procrastination. By doing things that you know contribute to you fulfilling your purpose or achieving your higher order goals and priorities, you continue motivating yourself to timely action and productivity. You'll be able to consistently accomplish the items on your to-do list.

Lack of discipline

Motivation may not necessarily be enough to prevent procrastination in some cases. It's because highly motivated people who lack self-discipline are all talk with no action. On the other hand, even an un-motivated person who is very disciplined will continue working on tasks regardless of how they feel. They don't procrastinate.

Unfortunately, self-discipline isn't something you can get in a 711 outlet. It takes time to acquire it. The sad fact is that the older we are, the harder it is to cultivate self-discipline. The good news however is that hope springs eternal and no matter how difficult it can be at an older age, it's still possible.

If you believe you need more discipline in working on the tasks in your to-do lists, you can give this technique a shot to help you overcome the very strong temptation to procrastinate. Think of the single worst possible consequence of failing to accomplish a task on time, if not at all, due to procrastinating. Then, think of the single greatest possible pleasure you can experience by not procrastinating. Yes, it may not be as powerful as developing self-discipline but it's a very good alternative while still in the process of doing so.

Being lazy

Most people procrastinate due to exhaustion, be it mental or physical. It makes getting out of ruts more challenging because when exhausted, staying in a state of rest requires little or no effort at all compared to getting yourself moving again. When this becomes chronic or persistent, it develops into laziness, which makes even the lightest of tasks in a to-do list weigh like a ton. This eventually leads to procrastination, which fans the flame of laziness even more and becoming a crazy downward spiral of unproductivity.

There's only one way to put the brakes on this crazy downward spiral: action! Some of the most beneficial ways to act and beat laziness is regular exercise like lifting weights at the gym, running or biking – all of which help increase energy levels for breaking the stronghold of laziness.

Believe it or not, poor diet can also lead to laziness. If you eat a lot of simple and sugary carbohydrates, you'll suffer often from sugar spikes and crashes, which result in low energy and sluggishness. It's best to replace these with more complex carbohydrates like brown rice and whole grains as well as mixing it up with some lean sources of protein so that you enjoy steady energy and not feel lazy.

Chapter 11 – Other Useful Tips for Maximizing Your To-Do List

"Being unable to say no can make you exhausted, stressed and irritable." – Auliq Ice

As the quote above says, not being able to say no can keep you from becoming productive. When you always say "yes", you eventually fill your plate to the brim – spilling over even. Eventually, you might burn out or worse, quit. From productivity, you may go down the path of unproductivity.

As one author once said, it takes a lot to say "no" if deep inside you really want to answer in the affirmative. You'll need to practice and master the art of saying no for personal productivity's sake, even if your guts want to scream "yes!" When you're able to do that, you can say yes to what's really important and productive. It frees up your time for more productive and higher order priorities.

One of the best ways to learn how to say no is to know what's really most important to you. When you know that and how saying yes to something that's not related to it can prevent you from your priorities, you can easily say no. If you know for example that the most important thing in the world for you is to be able to provide well for your family, saying "no" to a ski trip – even if it's all expenses paid and you've been dying to experience one – is easy to say if you know that it will keep you from finishing a task that will help you be promoted to manager.

Know your priorities and learn to say "no" for productivity.

Another way you can maximize your to-do lists is exercise. What? How's that even related, you may wonder. Well, hold on and let me explain.

First, exercising regularly helps optimize blood flow, which of course includes blood flow to the brain. When blood flow to the brain improves, so do cognitive performance, which can enable you to accomplish more in less time. By working smarter, you can accomplish more and improve personal productivity.

Next, exercising regularly helps increase your stamina, which in turn lets you manage your affairs better. When your stamina improves, you can do more things in your to-do list and as such, become more productive.

Lastly, exercising regularly keeps you in great shape. What does it have to do with your to-do list? Well, if you're in great shape, you feel good about yourself – you're in high spirits most of the time. As such, you're inspired to work hard and smart most of the time, allowing you to accomplish more tasks in your to-do list.

Lastly, eating right can help you maximize your to-do list as well. How? Eating healthy produces healthy cells, which is important for optimal mental and physical performance. You can function better and accomplish more simply by cleaning up your diet.

Consider for example how a diet that's chock full of sugar can affect mental performance. Such a diet results in frequent sugar spikes, which make you hyper, and crashes, the latter making you feel sleepy and sluggish. Imagine if you often feel high then feel sluggish within a few minutes? It'll slow you down both mentally and physically, taking you much longer to accomplish tasks and reduce your personal productivity.

Diets that are sorely lacking in important vitamins and minerals can cause your cognitive performance to take a dip. As a result, so will your ability to accomplish your tasks on time. For example, Vitamin B deficiency can result in poor nerve and neuron health and result in reduced mental performance. Of course, mental performance is often tied to the ability to get the items on your to-do lists done. Eating healthy foods at the right amounts together with proper supplementation can go a long way in improving your mental performance and allow you to accomplish more of the tasks in your to-do lists and in less time.

Conclusion

In this book, we have covered a lot of topics! From effective tactics to apps that will help you to organize your workload, this book has you covered. If needed, read it through again and remember to split your prioritizing into different times so that you know exactly what to work on. For example, the most productive time of your day is always going to be first thing in the morning and directly after a decent break. Those are times when you have more energy and focus, and that's when you should look at your to-do lists to make sure you start working on the most important tasks.

Your to-do list system is simplified using my methods because simple is often much easier for you to handle than trying to take on more complex software which can give you frustration. By working your notes into your to-do list at set intervals, answering mail at set intervals and dealing with all that bulky paperwork at one session, you actually divide your work into small units throughout the day whereby you get a lot more done. You also make it easier to keep track of events by having alerts and making sure that all items on the to-do list are segregated into small doable jobs, instead of huge undertakings that are mind-boggling!

The apps suggested in this book have been tested and tried and are what I would recommend you try. Although, there are many apps in the app store that you can try when you have some down time. The goal is to find one that suits you better than all the rest. Avoid the complex. The reason why you have so many problems with the amount of work that you have is because you already **make it too complex**. Make things simple. Don't use systems that make your workload even heavier. Believe me when I say that some systems are really so time consuming that they make your workload much heavier than it needs to be.

Above all, play around with alerts and make sure that when an alert comes up on your phone or your tablet, you act on it. Never dismiss it and tell yourself that you will remember, because in doing so, you are setting yourself up for potential failure. If you need to push it back, reschedule an alert for another time. If you have acted on it, then you don't need to use up that space in your memory that could be used for other things. When you get into a routine that works for you, try to get others within your work team on the same page so that you can simply transfer requests to them immediately from your phone when you need to. If you are all working on the same page, it cuts out all the hassle and makes sure that your day is every bit as productive as it can be.

Working can seem overwhelming at times and when it does, remember that the reason it may be overwhelming is that you are overthinking things and not delegating in the way that you need to. The more efficient your to-do system is, the more you can get done and that's a huge step in the right direction. Set up your system and you eventually take control. Your entries onto your to-do list and into your notes will become something that's so automated that you don't lose track of to-dos ever again, and can meet all your deadlines on time, with time left over for a nice cup of coffee. Then, you will know that you not only saved yourself time, but that you used the time that you had wisely.

So please, take what you've learned from this book to heart and set up to-do lists that can be managed efficiently! You'll thank yourself for it later. Here's to your success and I wish you the best!

Book 3

Time Management

How to Get Laser-Sharp Focus for Enhanced Productivity & Concentration

2nd Edition

Dane Taylor

Introduction

Have you ever wondered how others have such sharp focus and can achieve more than you? You know, those people who stand out from the crowd because they get things done. Don't you want to get onto the fast track too? I can't say I blame you if you do. We all struggle to keep up with the rat race, but sometimes our time management skills and lack of concentration get in the way of our road to success. If this sounds like you, don't worry. With this book, you will soon learn how to sharpen your concentration and achieve a level of productivity second to none. In no time at all, you too will be the person who stands out but for all the right reasons.

As 'How to Get Laser-Sharp Focus for Enhanced Productivity & Concentration' takes you on a journey of self-discovery, you will quickly understand where you have been falling short and learn how to implement change. You will discover new ways to improve your level of concentration. Your ability to target and overcome problems will also drastically improve. You will learn to focus your attention on details you had previously overlooked as you rushed through jobs or overlooked them because they posed too much of a challenge. You will find out how you can avoid interruptions that minimize your productivity, stealing as much as 6 hours of every working day! You will also learn to avoid procrastination, one of the main causes of lost business, income, and wages for workers today.

Within the chapters that follow, we share with you

productivity solutions that work, solutions that will suit your lifestyle, and solutions that have proven invaluable to the success of CEO's, entrepreneurs, and moguls worldwide. Divided into easy to locate subsections, these solutions are optimized not only for your reading pleasure, but also for your ability to later reference sections of interest with ease. As you begin reading, you will soon find that this organization method is not a coincidence: it is a simple method to help you to focus and target your personal problem areas as you begin to similarly restructure and organize your approach to productivity.

Chapter 1 – The Man on the Tightrope, The Alligator, The Wolf and The Baby

Picture a man standing on a tightrope. The tightrope is strung across a large canyon. The man isn't too worried because he knows that he has good balance and he has walked across a tightrope before. Then the man looks down. Below him, in a deep pool of water is a large alligator snapping its jaws. The man begins to sweat. As he lifts his eyes up to focus ahead, he can't help but think about the alligator below snapping its jaws. His heart begins to race and he begins to wobble slightly on the tightrope. Just as he is about to take a second step, he hears a deep growl behind him and he knows that it is a wolf. He doesn't turn around, but as he stands on the tightrope he can't help but hear the deep rumbling and gnashing of teeth. The alligator snapping, the wolf growling, and the need to maintain his balance all begin to weigh on the man. As he thinks about the what if of falling, the inability to turn back, and the necessity of keeping his balance, he begins to panic even more. Soon, the man finds himself stuck, he can make no progress forward for fear of falling and turning back and giving up is not an option. Just as he is about to give up all hope, the man sees a baby on the other side of the canyon. The baby is alone and crawling quite quickly towards the edge of the canyon. Suddenly, the man begins to shuffle forward. At first his pace is slow, but gradually he begins to take long strides and soon he is on the other side of the canyon with the child safely in his arms.

In the story above, the man succeeded in crossing the canyon, but why? And why couldn't he succeed before? As he stood on the tightrope, unable to move, the was fearful for his life just as he was fearful for the life of the child, but why, in one instance was he able to move forward and not in the other? The simple answer is – the human brain's capacity for multitasking.

The Thing About Multitasking...

When we ask the human brain to multi-task, or focus on multiple important items at once, we are dividing the resources that the brain has to work with. For example, as the man stood on the tightrope, he was focused not only on getting across the canyon, but he was also focused on the alligator below him and the wolf behind him. The more he concentrated on these other things, the less the man was able to concentrate on safely getting across the tightrope. On the other hand, however, when the man spotted the baby crawling to the edge of the canyon, his sole point of concentration was that baby. By focusing all of his effort on the child, the man crossed over the tightrope and saved the baby. Why? Because there were no distractions, nothing else stealing from his limited resources.

So, what does this story have to do with you...or anything else for that matter? Well, in the example above, the less points of focus that the man had, the more successful he was at making progress. The same concept applies to everyday office tasks. Although there are those who claim to be able to multi-task effectively, scientists disagree. The human brain can only fully concentrate on a limited amount of information at one time and when you multi-task you are asking the brain to exceed that limit. In other words, you are asking your brain to focus on the wolf, the alligator, and keeping your balance. When this happens, the result is a lack of progress. You may not find yourself facing down a tightrope, an alligator, and a wolf, but the same principle of concentration applies. If you try to complete your PowerPoint presentation, talking to your personal assistant about a meeting next week, and considering which job applicant to hire for a recent open position at your firm, you are simply asking too much of your brain. In order to make progress, you need to focus on the baby, the one project that requires your immediate attention. Once that project has been completed, you will have one project completed successfully and you will be able to focus on the next "baby."

This seems like a simple solution for making progress and managing time appropriately, so why isn't it? The problem with today's society is that we have convinced ourselves that we must focus on more than one thing. Obviously, not in the form of alligators and wolves, and not necessarily in the form of multiple business projects. How many times have you been in a meeting and heard a cell phone begin to ring? This is a common distraction in our day-to-day lives. Although we may not even realize that this is a distraction at all, it is taking away our ability to focus on the task at hand. This splintering of focus quickly shatters our concentration and detracts from our productivity. It turns our brain's attention to the alligator below while we try to force it to focus on the task at hand even while only 50% of its resources are free.

Why is all of this important? Well, research has shown that it takes twice as long for the human brain to focus on the main task at hand after an interruption or distraction. That means that if it took you ten minutes to begin writing your PowerPoint presentation to begin with, it will take you around twenty minutes to get back to writing after a distraction. When added up throughout the day, this twenty-minute period and the time spent focusing on other tasks during the day quickly takes away from productivity in the workplace. This distraction from productivity can be reflected in your ability to finish a single project due to making minimal progress on three projects or it can be reflected in poor quality work as a result of being pressed for time and being inattentive to detail as a result of split focus.

So, if the brain isn't capable of multitasking, yet we are faced with multitasking requests every single day, what can we do to ensure that those alligators and wolves don't steal our focus?

Keeping the Beasts at Bay, tricks for Improving Focus

The beasts of distraction are always going to be waiting just around the corner, so in order to maximize our productivity we need to anticipate their approach. There are a number of ways that we can do this, through sharpening our focus on primary tasks and through shutting out the lurking beasts of distraction. Let's take a look at how you can implement these tactics now.

Productivity Boosting Apps

A solid portion of the time that we waste daily is spent on smartphones, tablets, and computers, checking email, calling friends, answering texts, playing with apps, etc. So, if we are going to be glued to this technology for so much of the time, why not make our technology a tool for productivity rather than distraction?

There are a number of great smartphone / tablet / desktop applications that have been designed with business productivity in mind. While all of the apps that we are going to share below differ from each other in some way or another, they all share the common goal of improving concentration, focus, and business productivity. Let's take a look at the top five productivity apps.

1. Omnifocus – Omnifocus is one of the most highly recommended productivity apps. Available as a free app. as well as a pro. app., Omnifocus provides one platform for managing all aspects of life, however, it ensures that personal and business wires don't get crossed. Monitor projects, keep up with tasks, stay on top of to-do lists, remember travel plans, and know what every day holds before even getting started.

2. RescueTime – RescueTime is a free or premium paid app that has been utilized by some of the most successful companies out there. It claims to be able to "rescue" almost four hours of wasted time per person, per week by users utilizing it to voluntarily block out time wasting websites. RescueTime also has a time tracker so users can see just where their wasted time is going each day and use that information to block time wasting sites.

3. <u>Wrike</u> – Wrike is a project management system that is available as a free app or on a paid plan depending upon your needs. Wrike is an all in one system that helps to save time, increase focus, and increase productivity by keeping all relevant information for projects in one place. Avoid hopping around online and getting distracted because Wrike features time tracking, workload management, task management, a real-time news feed, integration of popular services like Dropbox and Google Drive, discussion capability, document collaboration services, and customized reporting.

4. <u>Sound Curtain</u> – Sound Curtain costs $4.99 and promotes productivity in the work environment through implementing a combination of white noise and harmonic sound. Utilizing this app with a headset drowns out excess noise in the office and prevents distraction so that you can get the job done.

5. <u>Cue</u> – A free app, Cue might have the appearance of a calendar and organizer app. but it's actually much more. More like your computer desktop, Cue organizes and links all of your network accounts, social media accounts, e-mail accounts, Dropbox account, Airline network information, and your calendar. Think of it as a personal organizer to organize your distractions so that you can knock them out all at once.

Medication and Supplementation

Medications and supplements aren't for everyone, particularly if you are currently on a medication regimen (in which case you should ALWAYS consult your doctor before adding any medications or supplements to your diet.) When medications and supplements are possible, however, they can help to keep the brain sharp, improve mental clarity, improve memory, and maintain full body health – all of which are key in optimal productivity in the workplace.

Piracetam

Piracetam is perhaps one of the most recommended supplement when it comes to improving productivity in the work place. Unlike prescription drugs, Piracetam is a non-prescription drug and has been utilized to boost brain power since 1978. Piracetam is a type of supplement known as a racetam. Racetams work through stimulating the receptors of acetylcholine in the brain. By prompting increased acetylcholine action in the brain, Piracetam improves concentration, increases memory recall, increases reaction times, and increases sensitivity to stimuli. An additional benefit of the racetam Piracetam is that it also has the ability to reduce anxiety, which in turn increased productivity in individuals who may otherwise be slowed by anxious feelings.

Dopamine Supplementation

Drugs that improve productivity by acting upon the neurotransmitter Dopamine, are prescription drugs and their use must always be monitored by a medical professional. With that said, for individuals suffering from dopamine impairment, these drugs can provide temporary increased productivity by increasing focus and energy. The stimulation of dopamine in the brain is the perfect answer to productivity troubles for some people, but it is always important to note that these types of drugs come with side effects. If you think that you may need a prescription dopamine supplement like Ritalin or Adderall, make sure you discuss the pros and cons of their use with your doctor. It is also necessary to discuss use of these types of drugs with employers in some cases because while they can improve performance, they can also create other undesirable effects which become a problem in jobs such as being a 787 pilot.

Circumin

Circumin is a natural ingredient found in the spice Turmeric. Circumin not only has antioxidant, anti-inflammatory, antibacterial, anti-viral, anti-cancer, and antifungal properties, but it also has been noted to increase serotonin and dopamine, to break down brain plaques associated with some neurodegenerative diseases, and to increase brain blood flow. All of these actions and properties contribute to better brain health which, in turn, contributes to improved productivity.

DHA

DHA or docosahexaenoic acid is an incredibly important supplement for the human brain, so much so that it is often included in baby formula. An omega-3 fatty acid, DHA is just one of the pieces that goes in to building the cerebral cortex of the brain – that it, the area that is responsible for attention, creativity, language, brain cell communication, motion, and memory.

Citocoline

Citocoline is a chemical found within the human brain. It plays many different roles including the reduction of inflammation, reduction of free radical damage, increasing brain energy, increasing plasticity in the brain, improving concentration, improving attention, improving focus, and increasing the levels of dopamine and acetylcholine in the brain naturally. Interestingly enough, citocoline has been utilized as a supplemental treatment by European doctors for years in the treatment of neurological disorders.

Acetyl-l-Carnitine

Acetyle-l-Carnitine, or ALC, is another amino acid that protects the brain from damage by free radicals through its antioxidant properties. ALC acts on the brain by increasing brain cell sensitivity to insulin which in turn allows them to more efficiently utilize glucose to fuel brain cell functioning. Not only does ALC work as a natural anti-depressant, but it also boosts mood, mental clarity, memory. Improves focus, and increases processing speed. These characteristics and ALC's fast acting properties make it a great go to for improving productivity.

Ginkgo Biloba

Ginkgo biloba has long been utilized in traditional medicine as a way to increase blood circulation as well as to protect the brain against damage from free radicals. For many years, ginkgo was also touted as having the ability to improve memory, however, more recent studies reveal that this may not be true. Whether this is true or not, though, there is no doubt that the circulatory and antioxidant properties of ginkgo are still beneficial enough to make this a great supplement for increasing overall productivity.

Vitamins

While in an ideal world all of us would eat a diet so varied that we didn't require a multi-vitamin supplement, this is not an ideal world. The truth is, is that we eat a diet heavy with grains, sugars, and proteins and one with very few fruits and vegetables. Even when we do eat fruits and vegetables, they are rarely varied and they're almost always so heavily cooked that there are few nutrients left in them. So, it becomes necessary for us to incorporate a high quality vitamin in to our daily diet.

You may be wondering just what a daily vitamin has to do with your ability to be productive. The answer is found in balanced nutrition, vitamin D, and Vitamin B. In order for our bodies to function optimally, they require certain vitamins and minerals that nourish cells, tissues, and organs. Without these vitamins and minerals in adequate quantities we begin to experience signs of deficiency. Vitamin deficiency symptoms depend upon the vitamin that is deficient, but common deficiencies that affect productivity through their impact on the brain include:

- B complex vitamins which assist in preventing signs of aging in the brain, prevent memory loss, help with clarity of thought, assist in the production of neurotransmitters
- Vitamin C, which is referred to many as the "memory vitamin." Vitamin C has been known to improve memory, increase IQ, fight signs of aging in the brain,

and suppresses the creation of cortisol – a hormone related to stress.

- Vitamin D, which helps to prevent cognitive decline associated with aging, improve our ability at solving problems, and improve memory.
- Vitamin E, which is known for its role in heart health, but is also commonly used to maintain brain health. Vitamin E is great at preventing age related mental decline.
- Vitamin K, which helps to maintain mental sharpness and improve memory (particularly for words.)

Popular Corporate Approaches for Improving Focus in the Workplace

Productivity apps, supplements, vitamins, and medications are great ways to sharpen focus, but so too are the corporate strategies we are about to look at. Below you will find some of the most reputable focus targeting strategies implemented in major corporations worldwide.

Work Most When You Work Best

In any working atmosphere, there are going to be times of the day when interruptions are fewer and times when they are more. By paying attention to this ebb and flow of distraction in your office, you will be able to take note of the times when your concentration and focus are most challenged. An understanding of this general schedule of distractions will allow you to better schedule your workload for each job on your task list. For example, if you have an important keynote speech to write that requires your full focus, you should schedule this during a time when the office is quietest – such as during lunch time while pushing your lunch hour to another time.

In one example of a business that implemented a similar tactic of time management, the most effective worker in the whole building actually worked late every night and came in very early every morning. His reasoning was simple - in the hours before other workers came into the office and before the phone started ringing, he was able to tackle the tasks that required his full attention. Then, when people came into the office, the tasks that remained were tasks that required less of his concentration and could be completed despite the presence of distraction. In the evening, he used an extra hour to assess the workload for the following day in complete silence, able to think of nothing else but the task at hand. This method of planning ahead also ensured productivity for the following day. Of course, not everyone is going to be ready or willing to work before or after work hours, but the principle remains the same. The most demanding tasks require scheduling during the times of least distraction so that focus can remain sharp, jobs can be completed successfully, and quality can be maintained.

Time Locks

Time locks are a rather simple tactic of eliminating any excessive distraction that takes place in the workplace and results in a lack of focus. So, just how does a "time lock" work? Instead of changing your schedule to work alongside distractions in the office, a "time lock" is an agreement of sorts with your boss or with the people that you work with, to prevent distractions. A time lock establishes a certain time of day when your office or desk is a "no go" area. During this time, your co-workers and your boss know that you are not to be disturbed barring an emergency. If you are worried that this approach will upset coworkers, then consider being open and honest with them. Discuss the complexity of the workload that you have on your plate and they will hopefully be able to see that you have a valid reason for making your office "off-limits" during certain times. To maintain the efficiency of a "time lock" period, ask your assistant to take your calls or, if you don't have an assistant, simply switch off your cell phone and turn down the ringer on your office phone.

Make sure that you allow yourself enough time to complete the tasks that you need to complete while the "time lock" period is active. Force yourself to focus solely on your project at hand. This method of approach allows you a specific period of "productive time" to get those more difficult jobs completed in silence and leaves the rest of your day to tackle those less tedious or complicated jobs.

A great application of the time lock tactic would be in an office where the payroll process is particularly complex. Enforcing a time lock where no one is permitted to contact anyone in the payroll department during the time when payroll is being cut, would prevent any distraction and possible error that could result from that distraction.

You can see from this example, that the "Time Lock" system works, but it only works if you plan ahead. Plan ahead for the work that you need to complete during this period and plan ahead to ensure that you won't need anything like refreshments during your time lock period. Then, all you need to do is to concentrate fully on the job at hand and you will find that your focus is optimal.

Break Down Long, Boring or Particularly Difficult Tasks

When facing a particularly long, boring, or difficult task, it is easy to lose focus. The longer you work on a particular task, the more frustrating it can become. Eventually, you will find yourself in a place where you are making no progress at all and your focus has been lost completely. You can avoid this happening by breaking down this type of task in to smaller time slots. For example, if you anticipate a project taking two hours, try breaking it up in to 30 minute increments. Not sure when to switch to another project or take a break? Let the content of your job dictate your break time. When you find yourself making less progress and becoming distracted easily, it's time to step away and come back when you are able to refocus. Just make sure that you don't allow yourself to get distracted when you take a momentary break.

Indulge Your Creativity

You may have noticed recent trends in large companies that provide a creative work atmosphere for employees. These companies offer napping pods, basketball courts, smoothie bars, fish tanks, and more, but why? These things encourage employees to loosen up and be more creative. This change in behavior not only improves the amount of creativity that goes in to jobs, but it also offers an outlet for stress. As stress is reduced and creativity is increased, it becomes easier to focus and remain dedicated to a project.

So what are you to do if your company doesn't offer these types of solutions? There is plenty that you can do to create your own creative outlets, even in the workplace. Utilize fidget toys, keep inspirational coffee table books in your office, take a walk around the office, hold a meeting in a local coffee shop, and involve games and social activities in projects. Any or all of these ideas will introduce a level of creativity in to projects increasing dedication to them by participants, as well as increasing your own focus as you break the "normal pattern" of activity.

Chapter 2 – Time Bandits

Much of being able to maintain your focus is being able to identify a time bandit and what to do when you do identify one. Much like general distractions around the office, time bandits beg for your attention and interrupt your concentration, making it more difficult to get back to the task at hand. What exactly is a time bandit, though? As the name suggests, a time bandit is anything that vies for the limited time in your schedule. A time bandit can be a coworker who drones on constantly about their newest boyfriend or most recent "disaster" in their dating life, it can be time around the water cooler, the boss who insists upon asking you to do their work for them, or that one website that you just can't help but visiting every hour. The one thing that all of these things have in common, is that they are all making demands on your attention and breaking your concentration.

Are time bandits really that big of a deal though? After all, a few minutes checking out that website for the newest sale items or a few minutes listening to the latest dating horror story from your coworker...they're not really that big of a deal are they? It's just a *few* minutes.

The truth is that yes; time bandits really are that big of a deal! If you spend eight hours a day at work and ten minutes of every hour giving in to a time bandit, that's eighty minutes (or an hour and twenty minutes) every hour that you are not working. An hour and twenty minutes that you could be using to draw up that contract, write that speech, or finish that proposal. It's an hour and twenty minutes that you won't have to work overtime or at home in order to finish up those projects that go unfinished, because "time bandits" just aren't going to fly as an excuse for why you didn't meet your monthly numbers...

Is time all that we lose when we allow time bandits in to our lives, though? What about concentration? When we allow time bandits in to our professional lives, we not only lose that ten minutes every hour, but we also break our concentration from current projects. This break in concentration causes a loss of fluidity in our work as well as adding a further delay when we return to the project at hand and have to reorient ourselves to the item that we were working on. So, what can we do to avoid succumbing to these time bandits? How can we maintain our concentration while at work and not give in to those distracting websites, co-workers, and water cooler conversations?

In the last chapter, we talked about using techniques like "time locking" to eliminate distractions in the office and avoid interruptions. This is a technique that proves particularly effective when a distraction is controllable as in the co-worker or boss who continually interrupts your workflow. Time locking allows you to maintain control of your schedule by putting limitations on others. This method of improving focus doesn't always work on time bandits, however, since some time bandits are self-imposed. We choose to visit that website and waste time, we choose to check our email a little too regularly, we choose, to allow our concentration to be diverted. So how can we enforce the practice of time locking upon ourselves? Throughout the rest of this chapter we will take a look at some proven methods of reducing or eliminating those pesky self-imposed time bandits.

Implement Distraction Reduction Apps

When we talked about losing focus in the workplace as a result of distractions, we introduced the idea of utilizing apps for the smartphone, tablet, and computer. Fortunately, there are also a good number of apps that are designed to help to manage personal distraction as well as improve focus in the office. These apps work by altering current habits, establishing new habits, and enforcing self-control.

1. Freedom – A free or premium app for your phone and computer, Freedom is designed to eliminate web surfing and app based distractions all together. By blocking apps and websites for specific periods of time, Freedom improves concentration and eliminates the chance of broken concentration as a result of self-imposed time bandits!

2. Isolator – Designed to improve focus, Isolator is a free tool that hides all icons and windows except for the one being worked on. This helps you to avoid clicking on that email button "one more time," since you can't even see the email button! Isolator is a simple work environment software, but it is one of the few that works with Windows and Mac. If you work on Max. you will find Think, Quiet, and Haze Over to all be similar and Mac specific.

3. Focus Booster – Available with free and premium plans, Focus Booster is an app that is designed to help you to take control of your work time by scheduling tasks in 25 minute (or longer/shorter) time slots. After each time slot, a short break is permitted before moving on to the next time slot.

This app gives no room for wasting time and a great sense of satisfaction for task completion.

4. <u>Stay on Task</u> – A free or premium app, Stay on Task is designed to keep users on task in a gentler way than the more aggressive distraction reducing apps. Similar to having a mother standing over your shoulder, Stay On Task works by checking in at scheduled times to ensure that you are still on track with your currently scheduled tasks.

5. <u>Stickk</u> – An unusual, but particularly effective, app in the world of preventing distraction and improving concentration on relevant tasks is Stickk. The idea behind this service is betting on your own success. Users literally set a goal, put up the stakes, pull a referee on to your "case" and even add friends for added support. The aim of the game is to have fun while pushing for increased productivity.

Popular Business Approaches for Minimizing Distractions and Improving Concentration

In the first chapter, we took a look at business tactics designed to improve focus and thereby increase productivity. As it happens, there are also a good number of these types of approaches designed to minimize distractions in the workplace as well. In this section we are going to take a look at a few of them.

Set Up Times to Address Work Related Distractions

Improve your concentration on tasks in the minute by scheduling times in the day to work on work related distractions. Rather than checking e-mail regularly throughout the day and wasting ten minutes here and there, schedule a short period at the beginning and end of the day to catch up on e-mail correspondence. This type of approach is called proactive working, where you already have a plan in place to tackle work-related distractions rather than allowing the distractions to dictate your schedule and interrupt your flow of concentration.

Identify and Minimize Visual Distractions

Just as technology can distract us from tasks at hand and steal our time away, so too can visual distractions. In order to avoid visual distractions in the workplace pay attention to your immediate environment. Remove "fidget" items from your desk, close your door if you are apt to be distracted by co-workers in the hallway, consider moving to a solitary quiet space to improve concentration on a particular task, and make sure to keep an organized desk space to prevent the distraction of clutter. While these types of time bandits may not stop by your desk for a discussion, they can certainly leach from your available work time and destroy your concentration.

Make Use of Window Blinds

This may seem like a peculiar piece of advice, however, if you have ever worked in an office with a view, then you know just how valuable window blinds can be. By nature, most of us are "people watchers" and as such we are easily sucked in to watching life unfold before our eyes. This is particularly true when we can do this from a position of power, giving ourselves a Godlike position over others. This distracting people watching can quickly whisk away hours of the day if we allow it, so we recommend using window blinds. If you can't see something to be distracted by it, you can't be distracted by it! It really is as simple as that.

Be Realistic in What You Can Tackle Daily

As we mentioned back in chapter 1, we are much more likely to allow distractions when we become bored with the work that we are doing. We are also much more likely to allow distractions when we set unobtainable goals for ourselves. In an effort to avoid this, try setting up your to do list the night before and make sure that you are not overtaxing yourself. We all have jobs that must be completed daily, but when we overcommit and overschedule, we can become overwhelmed and give in to distraction much more easily. So what is a reasonable amount of work? Well, that really depends upon where you work, what you do for work, and the tasks that you need to get completed on any given day. You know your working speed and you should know from looking at a to do schedule when you have taken on too much.

Implement a Routine

You may or may not have heard of the 40:15:5 routine. A time management tactic, 40:15:5 refers to the amount of time dedicated to specific tasks. For 40 minutes you will work on a task without giving in to distraction. Then, for 15 minutes you can check your e-mail, texts, social networks etc. so long as they are work related. Then lastly, for 5 minutes, allow yourself to recover from the past 55 minutes. Walk around, stretch your legs, take in sights other than your immediate working area, and take care of any needs you might have. Just remember, that your 5 minutes is not necessarily your coworkers 5 minutes, so don't distract them just because you are taking advantage of your break period in your schedule.

Chapter 3 – Why Do Today...?

People quip, "Why do today what you can do tomorrow?" and while it may be a joke, there is plenty of truth in the saying. That is not to say that it's a constructive way of thinking, but it's a common way of thinking. A vast majority of people believe in procrastination as a technique for tackling life and everything it brings with it. The truth was best spoken by actor Christopher Parker, however, when he said that "procrastination is like a credit card: it's a lot of fun until you get the bill." Just like tasks that we push off due to distractions, lack of focus, and lack of concentration, procrastination is simply another way of making today less productive and tomorrow more demanding.

Each and every day, most of us sit down to begin working and we start by making a list or at least reviewing the tasks that we need to do for the day. When you are someone who allows procrastination to take hold, however, you begin your day regretting the things that you did not do yesterday. You face a list that overflows with not only the tasks of today, but the tasks of yesterday as well. Starting the day in this way is not just overwhelming, but it is also distracting as you find yourself focusing on the tasks of yesterday and the topics of today. The question is, however, is there anything that we can do to effectively eliminate procrastination in order to succeed in our professional lives?

Why Do People Procrastinate?

Before we take a look at some of the corporate skills used to avoid procrastination, let's first take a look at why procrastination is such a common practice. Why do people put things off? The reason for procrastinating tasks can be varied and depend upon many factors, but the truth is that we procrastinate simply because we don't want to complete a task. Sure, the details behind not doing that task might be the result of any range of factors, but ultimately it all comes down to a lack of desire. "But I was busy…" you might say. Well, "busy" is nothing more than an excuse for a lack of desire, drive, or motivation. The point is, a task was to be done yesterday and you did not do it. In order to be successful in business or, in fact, in any area of life, you must stop procrastinating, you must find a way to complete today's tasks today and leave tomorrow open for tomorrow.

So, we must ask again, is there anything we can do to effectively eliminate procrastination in order to succeed in our professional lives?

How Do the Successful Do It?

A great model to look at when considering how you can stop procrastinating is that of the more successful business moguls. What do these men and women do to avoid procrastinating tasks? How do they ensure that by the end of the day, all tasks for that day have been put to bed? Let's take a look at some of the commonly used tactics by powerful CEO's and entrepreneurs worldwide.

Delegation

A very common tactic of avoiding procrastination among successful businessmen and women worldwide is delegation. Rather than simply putting off a task that may be unpleasant or out of their depth, these individuals delegate the task to someone who is capable of completing it themselves. Of course, this someone isn't just anyone, it's someone who enjoys or who is skilled at the task they are being asked to do. In delegating responsibility this way, these businessmen and women are freeing up their schedule to work on other tasks while ensuring that other less appealing tasks still get completed on time. Delegation is what most business owners refer to when they say that you must "work smart, not work hard."

Asking an Expert

If a task isn't something that can be completely delegated, it is, perhaps, something that can be tackled with help from another individual. Bringing on a partner to tackle tasks that are trying, that are out of your area of expertise, or that are simply too overwhelming to tackle alone, is a great way to ensure that the task still gets completed in a timely manner.

Tackle the Trying Tasks First

Another commonly used method of avoiding procrastination by successful businessmen and women is to prioritize jobs. When looking at the jobs that need to be completed for the day, these individuals always make it a point to tackle the more trying tasks first. Why? Well, think about your level of energy and concentration when you first get to the office in the morning. That afternoon sugar crash hasn't hit yet and the hunger pangs of late morning aren't vying for your attention.

Making it a point to take on the more difficult tasks during this time when you have more focus and more energy is the best way to seamlessly complete your entire to do list. You see, by getting the more arduous tasks off your plate first thing in the morning, you free up your afternoon to tackle the less demanding jobs – jobs that don't require excessive time or brain power. By utilizing this approach, you are not only getting jobs done, but you are also optimizing your resources to ensure that they get done properly.

Concentration Levels Throughout the day

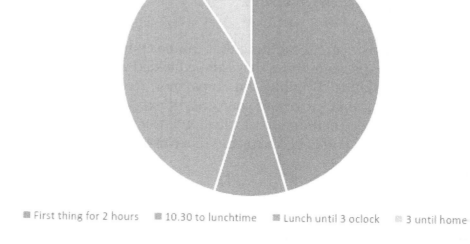

First thing for 2 hours   10.30 to lunchtime   Lunch until 3 oclock   3 until home

Implement Procrastination Reduction Apps

In addition to the problem solving tactics noted above, there are, of course, a number of apps for smartphones, tablets, and computers, that are designed to eliminate procrastination from your life. Taking advantage of these apps will give you that extra push that is needed to tackle those tasks that you can't delegate, but really don't want to complete.

1. <u>Procraster</u> – Available for $0.99, Procraster is a unique app designed to eliminate procrastination through the use of deadlines, rewards for met deadlines, productive time monitoring, and even prompts designed to help you get to the bottom of problems when you find yourself "stuck." This really is the ultimate in procrastination reduction apps.

2. <u>Beat Procrastination</u> – Available for $2.99, the Beat Procrastination app is designed to eliminate procrastination by getting to the root of the problem. Instead of simply telling you to "do better" or pressuring you with deadlines, this app. utilizes hypnotherapy to modify behavior so that procrastination becomes a thing of the past.

3. <u>Checker Plus for Google Calendar</u> – Checker Plus for Google Calendar is a free tool that scans your Google Calendar to determine how much time is available before the next upcoming event. This then provides you with an estimated timeframe for completing tasks on your to do list so that you can properly schedule tasks so that they can be finished before the next event on your calendar. This app is all about making the most of the time that you have available so that you can slot tasks in to appropriate time spans to get them finished.

4. <u>Chronos</u> – This is a free app that has the appearance of a time tracking software, but that offers so much

more than that. Unlike other basic time tracking software options that discourage procrastination through awareness of time use, Chronos focuses on discouraging procrastination by encouraging you to meet goals. Pictorial and infographic dashboards encourage tasks that range from meeting work goals, to sleeping more during the week.

5. Finish – A free app that targets tasks that need completion, Finish utilizes thorough "to do list" creation. This app promotes the use of task compilation, the use of time limits, and best of all, it avoids overwhelming lists by focusing primarily on the immediate tasks at hand.

Life Changes to Beat Procrastination

Apps are a great tool to provide that nudge to get moving on tasks that you have been procrastinating on. The truth is, however, is that procrastination is a bad habit and like any other bad habit, in order to break it, you must first change the way that you behave. It sounds quite difficult, but there are actually some relatively easy life changes that you can make to facilitate better working habits when it comes to procrastination.

1. Make Lists - Lists are one of the best tools that you can have to help you to avoid procrastination. Whether you use apps or a basic pen and paper, making to do lists help you to visualize what it is that you need to complete. Lists will also help you to prioritize what needs to be done so that you can better make use of your energy levels throughout the day.

2. Surround Yourself with Successful Achievers – When you surround yourself with people who strive for success and who know the importance of working hard today to provide for tomorrow, you set yourself up for success as well. Not only can you learn tips and seek advice from these successful people, but you can also benefit from a better overall mind frame.

3. Find a Role Model – You can promote an "acting now" frame of mind by locating a role model who has already achieved the goals that you are striving for. Not only will these individuals be able to help guide you through overcoming obstacles, but they will also serve as encouragement to stop procrastinating and act now in order to achieve your own success.

4. Become a "Doer" – There are two types of people in the world, those who do and those who don't. If you want to succeed in business, then you have to become a "doer." Stop wasting time and allowing yourself to make excuses for why you can't do something and instead, just find a way to do it! You can start small by implementing this tactic in your home life, for example, instead of putting dirty dishes in the sink, just unload the dishwasher and put the dirty dishes in there instead. It takes just as long to think of reasons why not to do something as it does to just do it.

Popular Business Approaches for Reducing Procrastination

Of course, personal change is the root of eliminating

procrastination for good, but so too is having the right tools for optimizing your work time, targeting your focus, and reducing procrastination. Many successful businessmen and women turn to tools and strategies to achieve their success. Let's take a look at some of these tactics now.

The Two Minute Rule

Based upon a book by David Allen called "Getting Things Done," the "two-minute rule" follows the basic principle of "if it takes less than two minutes, do it now." This idea is designed to avoid procrastinating smaller tasks that will take longer to complain about doing than it would take to actually do the task. When you follow this simple rule, you can easily knock the basic tasks off your everyday to do list so that you can concentrate more on the larger projects you still have to tackle.

One Project at a Time

This is a concept we have already touched upon when talking about optimizing focus. A strategy that is particularly common for successful businessmen and women is to tackle only one project at a time. While this improves focus and promotes successful completion of that task, it also helps to eliminate the feeling of being overwhelmed which is what commonly contributes to procrastination.

The Importance of Deadlines

Deadlines are crucial to the successful completion of any project. Without setting a deadline for a task you are giving yourself free reign to postpone that task for as long as you desire. If a project does not have an actual deadline, create one yourself and set up reminders to make sure that you don't forget about your deadlines when they are approaching.

Bite Sized Pieces

When faced with a ridiculously overwhelming task, we tend to want to run and hide. A tactic that is commonly utilized in corporations to overcome this fear response is to cut those tasks in to bite sized pieces. When we create "steps" or "milestones" for tasks we automatically make them less overwhelming and we are less likely to run...or in this case, procrastinate. Small bite sized pieces of any task are easier to focus on, faster to complete and are also a great way to track progress!

Reward Progress

A basic concept, but one that has proven to work over and over again is rewarding progress. This principle is just as applicable when it comes to rewarding yourself as it is when rewarding others. When success is rewarded, we not only feel accomplished, but we subconsciously condition ourselves to continue making progress in order to be rewarded again. So, if you're looking for a great way to not only increase focus on projects, but to also discourage procrastination, start rewarding   action!

Chapter 4 – The Body-Mind Connection

In chapter 1, we talked briefly about how the function of the brain influences our ability to focus. This is not the only way in which the mind and body are connected, however. Every task that we undertake involves a reliance upon our body to complete that task successfully. From physically carrying out tasks, to the ability to sit still and concentrate on a task, the connection between our body and mind plays a significant role in our success. It is for this reason that maintaining mental and physical health is a necessity when it comes to dominating the workplace. Your focus, your concentration, and your success are all dictated by how well you care for yourself.

Understanding the Basics

Most of us already understand the basic concept of our health impacting our success, for example, when we have the flu we are less able to concentrate on tasks and are therefore unsuccessful when it comes to completing that task. In the same way that our bodily health influences our ability to function, so too does our mental health. For example, when grieving or depressed, we find ourselves preoccupied and unable to concentrate on tasks, let alone succeed in completing them! In order to truly succeed, we must achieve, maintain, and monitor our physical and mental health. The healthy body is less of a distraction from success and a healthy mind is better able to focus, solve problems that arise, and complete tasks.

A Human Energy Crisis

Have you ever noticed how you feel after eating Thanksgiving dinner? This is an extreme example of a human energy crisis. This is the result of overeating, eating too many refined and unhealthy foods, and the resulting spike and consequential drop in blood sugar. The same thing happens to a lesser degree when we make poor eating choices and allow our health to slide.

Just like cars, our bodies demand fuel to make them run. The healthy body that is fueled by healthy foods is able to function optimally, but when the body is not healthy or is provided poor quality fuel, it is not able to function optimally. When the body is not functioning optimally and we are still attempting to put demands of the healthy body upon it, we find ourselves in an energy crisis. This crisis leaves us feeling tired, sluggish, mentally dull, and achy and as a result our work performance suffers.

Impaired Brain Functioning

When we eat poorly and do not provide our bodies with healthy and longer lasting nutrients (think, complex carbohydrates,) we experience frequent spikes and drops in blood sugar levels. These spikes and drops in blood sugar slow down the brain's ability to function and more specifically, impair memory and prevent learning. In addition, research by UCLA in 2012 even showed that high levels of certain sugars damages connections between brain cells, impairing communications and thus impairing cognition.

The brain requires healthy nutrition in order to function optimally. This means natural foods that are high in vitamin and mineral content and complex carbohydrates that are slower to break down in the digestive system. This also means eating smaller portions of foods in order to prevent a diversion of energy to the breakdown of nutrients.

It is not only the foods that we eat that influence our brain function, however. Our overall health also plays a significant part in optimal brain function as well. Of course, there are some health factors that we have minimal control over, but there are also plenty that we can control. For example, the amount of sleep we get, the amount of physical activity we take part in, dehydration, the extent to which we allow stress to impact our lives, and our ability to maintain a work/life balance. All of these things play a significant part in our ability to focus and succeed in our business life. Few people don't know how to address these concerns, the problem is, that most people don't want to address them because of the time it takes, the effort it takes, and the simple fact that we tend to get complacent.

So, what can you do to improve your brain function and energy use in order to improve your concentration and focus in the workplace?

Implement Healthy Living Management Apps

A steady increase in the use of technology has led to the

development of some great healthy living management apps. These apps help users to increase their performance, time management, and nutrition and best of all, they present a picture of progress. Let's take a look at some of the most frequently used apps for healthy living management.

1. My Fitness Pal – Free for download, the My Fitness Pal app is designed to track calorie intake, nutrient intake, exercise tracking, weight tracking, and it provides a supportive community for encouragement. This app is an all-around health focused app that tracks physical health and nutrition awareness to promote a healthier lifestyle.

2. Waterlogged – A free app for the iOS platform, Waterlogged is simple to use and allows you to track your water intake throughout the day. Utilizing this app is also a great way to encourage yourself to drink more water through goal setting! Water consumption is not only imperative to avoid dehydration, but it is also necessary to maintain mental clarity, concentration, and focus.

3. Mindbody – Free to use, Mindbody is an app designed to serve as a directory for full fitness. Simply put your zip code in to the app and you can locate various fitness studios, gyms, classes, and wellness resources local to you. In addition to providing references to these resources, this app also features special offers and deals. Mindbody encompasses it all in terms of full body health.

4. Lantern – Lantern is a rather costly app that works on a subscription service model, but if you find yourself struggling with mental balance, it is a great go to app. Focused on cognitive behavioral therapy techniques, this app serves as a full time companion

to help you to maintain the mental balance you need to succeed.

5. <u>Deep Sleep with Andrew Johnson</u> – Deep Sleep costs $2.99 to download, but is one of the highest recommended sleep apps out there today. Focusing on guided meditation as a technique to induce restful sleep, Deep Sleep optimizes your rest time to optimize your work time.

Life Changes to Improve Your Health

Apps are a great way to monitor progress when it comes to healthful living, but when it all comes down to it, your health is dependent upon your life choices. Whether you are a powerful CEO or an aspiring entrepreneur, your health is your responsibility. The effort you put in to maintaining your health will reflect in your ability to succeed on the job, so let's take a look at what you can do to put forth that effort.

1. Be conscious of your food choices – Mindfulness of your energy levels and your ability to perform on the job mean being aware of the foods that you choose to eat. Processed foods and unhealthy foods are easily accessible, particularly when they are sitting on the table in the breakroom, but in order to maximize your potential you must make healthier foods more accessible.

2. Increase your water consumption – Drinking more water throughout the day will keep you hydrated and more alert, but it will also keep you from overeating and turning to easily accessible junk food. How? Well, a significant portion of the time

when you feel that you are hungry, you are actually thirsty and mistaking that sensation of thirst for hunger.

3. Increase your physical activity – Physical activity is a necessary "evil" to maintain full body health. Physical activity does not necessarily mean that you have to hit the gym for hours at a time, however, it can include simple small changes that just get you up and moving! Try standing at your desk, taking the stairs instead of the elevator, and parking further away from work to get more steps in each day.

4. Stay on top of your physical and mental health – Regular checkups and "maintenance" care for your physical and mental health might seem like an inconvenience, but it is your responsibility to stay on top of these things. The healthier you are, the abler you are to meet your maximum potential in the workplace.

5. Relax! – Being overworked and overstressed quickly lead to poor performance on the job due to poor mental health. It is imperative that you take your mental health balance in to consideration when you evaluate your working schedule. Ensure that you build relaxation and time away from work in to every single day and you will notice an increase in your mental clarity and sharpness.

6. Pay attention – We're not talking about paying attention to work here, we are talking about paying attention to your health. When your body tells you that something is wrong, whether through pain, fatigue, or something more significant, pay attention. Don't allow your work life distract from your need to care for yourself. You may lose a day or

even a week by addressing health concerns, but failure to address a health concern or working while ill can result in far worse problems.

Chapter 5 – All Eyes Ahead

Your overall health is crucial to your success in the workplace, but so too is maintaining your focus. One of the best ways to do this is through setting goals and sticking to them. Goals not only serve as milestones on the way to success, but they also serve to improve focus and concentration by providing a set accomplishment to strive for. When we work with just a general idea of what we want to accomplish, we have only a far off point on the horizon to look toward. By setting milestones and goals to strive for, we encourage ourselves to succeed by making tasks more manageable and by allowing us to become more focused on the parts of the whole.

There are many ways that we can utilize goal setting behaviors to grow in the workplace. We can use goals to break down larger tasks to more manageable parts, we can use goals to maintain momentum when taking on mundane tasks, we can use goals to provide more concentrated resources to tasks through breaking them down in to smaller parts, and we can use goals to simply break up our day in to efficient segments.

Implement Goal Achieving Apps

In the previous chapters, we have talked about how apps can really help to improve concentration, focus, and time management skills in the office. Apps can also play a significant role in setting and achieving goals at work as well. By implementing these types of apps in to your business life, you help to sharpen your focus not only by creating a "list" of items to tackle, but you do so in a way that allows you to attack smaller goals in a progressive manner which facilitates success.

1. Nozbe – Nozbe is a free and premium task management app that is designed to increase your productivity by setting goals and creating milestones within those goals to increase your performance. If you are looking to really focus on completing jobs thoroughly and giving them the attention that they deserve, then this is the ideal app for you to start with.

2. IRunURun – IRunURun is a free and premium app that utilizes goals to promote goals by creating a game out of goal achievement. Users strive to meet a perfect 100 score by meeting the goals that they set for the week, but failure to meet goals subtracts from that score, pushing you to try better next time.

3. Goals on Track – Goals on track is both a goal setting and personal productivity app. A membership based program, Goals on Track provides a visual layout of goals, goal progress, and action plans to help you to better understand how to work "smarter" to achieve your goals.

4. Coach.me – If you are pushed for space on your mobile device, Coach.me might be just what you need. This free app provides coaching for productivity, weight loss, and general fitness by using goal setting behaviors and providing "cheerleaders" to push you on your way.

5. Goal Setting Workshop + Goal & Habit Tracker – This free app provides everything you need to get started on setting up goals for your personal

development and career. Brainstorm goals, commit to your resolutions and build the motivation to achieve the goals that you have set through this motivating app.

Popular Corporate Strategies for Goal Achievement

Many professional businessmen and women utilize apps to set, track, and achieve their goals in their personal and professional lives. In addition to utilizing apps, however, these successful individuals also implement various corporate strategies for achieving or enhancing these elements of success. Let's take a look at some of the more popular corporate approaches to goal achievement.

Focus on a Singular Goal at a Time

Previously we have emphasized the importance of breaking tasks down in to "bite sized pieces." We have also touched upon the importance of maximizing focus as much as possible. When you break tasks down in to smaller goals and focus on just one smaller goal at a time, you are giving your full attention to one building block of a final structure and increasing your accuracy for the whole project. Doing this means that your smaller goals and tasks are going to be completed more successfully and lead to faster and more efficient achievement of your final goal.

Reassessment

The ability to pause and reassess goals is necessary for anyone undertaking a task. As we progress through the smaller milestones of our goals, we often reveal elements that we did not anticipate previously, so it becomes necessary to reassess and adjust our plans and our final goals in order to succeed. If we do not reassess and adjust our plans in this way, we may find that we have wasted a lot of time and failed at achieving our final intended goal.

Utilize the S.M.A.R.T Approach

S.M.A.R.T stands for Specific, Measurable, Attainable, Relevant, and Time-bound. This approach to goal setting focuses on how to make goals achievable by creating them utilizing these five criteria.

In order to succeed, your goals must be specific in nature and answer a who, what, where, when, which, or why question.

Your goals must also be able to be measured. If you can't measure your progress towards your goal and the ultimate results of your completion of the goal, how are you going to know if your goal has been achieved?

Your goals must also be realistic, or attainable. Setting goals that are unachievable is only setting yourself up for failure and wasting your time in the process!

Your goals must be relevant, or have value to your business or current project.

Your goals must be time-bound, or be on a deadline.

By utilizing this approach to goal setting and goal achievement, you are creating a better understanding for yourself of the task at hand, but you are also setting out a path toward attaining your final goal.

Reference Locke and Latham

Locke and Latham are known for their 5 principles of goal setting in which they define how to set out clear goals that can be accomplished. The Locke and Latham approach emphasizes

Clarity, Challenge, Commitment, Feedback, and Task Complexity.

In order to be achievable, a goal must be clearly defined. Having clear goals let you know exactly what you are striving for so that you can direct your focus towards achieving it.

In order to be successful, goals must also be challenging. Setting challenging goals serves to motivate us to try to achieve them where setting more easily achievable goals requires little of us in terms of action.

In order for a goal to work well, we must have a commitment to it. If we set a goal that we have no commitment to, we are less likely to strive to meet that goal. Instead, set goals that you can commit to, goals that, for one reason or another, matter to you.

In order for goals to be attained, we must also seek advice and feedback. In order to accurately measure our progress towards a goal, it is necessary to seek feedback and advice from others who can let us know if we are beginning to stray from our original path. Advice and feedback are also a great way to measure whether we are just spinning our wheels and wasting time.

Lastly, in order for goals to be achievable, they must not be too complex. If you have a task that seems too complex, consider breaking it down in to smaller goals, or consider taking another route to achieve it. When we create goals that are too complex, we tend to overwhelm ourselves and this leads to burnout and lack of concentration.

Work on Establishing Objectives and Key Results

A very simple approach to goal setting and goal achievement is to work on establishing objectives and the key results that we expect to get from those objectives. For goals to be functional, we need first to set down the objective of that goal – what is it that we are attempting to do? What is the final product that we want to develop? Once we have established our objectives, we must then take a look at the key results that we hope to attain. These key results are based upon the objectives. For example, our objective with setting a goal may be to create a more productive structure to our HR department. The key results that we hope to see from this objective may be 50% improved interaction between general employees and the HR department.

The purpose of setting OKR's is to outline goals, the purposes of those goals, and to create a simplified picture of how goals can be utilized to achieve success.

Chapter 6 – How Motivation Impacts Focus

While goal setting is a great method of successfully completing tasks and making them more manageable, they get us nowhere if we are not motivated to achieve them. Motivation is something that may be lacking for any number of reasons, but when you find a way to increase your motivation in the workplace, you also find a way to increase your level of focus. Improving your performance through self-motivation is a powerful and well-established trait in a large percentage of successful businessmen and women worldwide, but just how do they go about it? Let's take a look at the impact of motivation on focus and success and then discuss the methods that worldwide moguls use to make motivation work for them.

What is Motivation?

Before we begin looking at how motivation impacts your ability to focus on and achieve goals, we must first understand what motivation is. In its very basic form, motivation is the driving force behind our success, it is what pushes us to strive for achievement. Without motivation we tend not to care whether we meet goals, in fact, we may not even set goals at all! Without motivation, we lack focus and without motivation, we fail to succeed. Think about it, have you ever seen a successful CEO of a major company who just didn't care about their company, their company's success, or their company's image in the media? Rarely does it happen. Why? Because these CEO's are motivated to care about all of these things because their success hinges on their company's success.

The Connection Between Motivation and Focus

The relationship between motivation and focus is a reciprocal one. Without an appropriate level of motivation, we are very unlikely to focus on a task. You see, by our very nature, we need a reason to do things, whether that reason is pending financial success, or simply feeling good about completing a task, without that driving force, we are unlikely to focus on success. Contrariwise, without giving a task adequate focus, we are unlikely to be motivated to complete it. For example, if we have a task that has been sitting on the corner of our desk for months we are not likely to be motivated to complete that task because, after all, it has waited this long already. By not setting a due date for completion of that task or creating milestones to lead to its completion, we are not giving ourselves the motivation that we need to focus on taking action.

Implement Motivating Apps

Just as apps can serve as a great way to create, track, and monitor progression when it comes to goals, they can also play an influential role in motivation as well. There are plenty of motivating apps out there to try, but here are some of our favorites.

1. BeeMinder – BeeMinder adds a little extra something to the concept of motivation. This free app promotes completion of goals and tasks by having you set goals and wager a real monetary

amount on your ability to complete these goals. Now, you don't get paid if you do complete your goals, but you do have to pay if you don't meet them! Is there any better way to get people to make progress than to ask them to put their money where their mouth is?

2. Unstuck – Another free app, Unstuck is an app designed to help you to overcome those moments when you just feel "stuck." This app focuses on promoting your motivation through peer and digital coaching and problem solving.

3. Happier – Happier is a free positivity app that focuses on boosting happiness levels in order to motivate you. Happier works by having you collect "happy moments" that occur throughout the day so that you can reflect upon them and use them as motivation as well as to improve your overall mood. A positive attitude goes a long way in motivating us to reach our goals, no matter how unreachable they may seem.

4. Headout– Headout is a free app that focuses on experience as a great motivator. We have already discussed how important it is to take a step away from work once in a while and Headout capitalizes on that concept. By listing local events and locations that you can head out to, this app gives you ideas to get away so that you can come back with renewed motivation to meet your goals.

Other Tactics for Improving Motivation

Apps are a great starting point for improving your level of motivation. It is important to note as well, however, that sometimes in order to improve our motivation, we must make changes to our lives as well. These changes can be challenging or even quite simple, but one thing is guaranteed, making any one of them will increase your motivation and improve your focus on success.

Practice Positivity

The way we look at things has a lot to do with how motivated we are in our lives. If we continually view the world through the eyes of a pessimist, we are always going to focus on the negative and find reasons not to do the things that matter. Overcome this negativity by practicing positivity throughout your day. Find one positive thing in everything that you do and soon enough you will notice that you are more motivated to work hard, achieve your goals, and succeed.

Utilize Visualization

Visualizing our success is the perfect way to focus our attention on why we are working so hard. Take a few moments out of every day and visualize yourself achieving the goals that you are striving to reach. What does your life look like at this point? What do you feel like? Revel in the sense of satisfaction that you will achieve and use this feeling to propel you forward in completing your task.

Try Resetting

Everyone at some point loses their focus. We become too

wrapped up in the daily comings and goings of life that we begin to feel lost and when that happens, we lose motivation. When you find yourself having this type of experience, step away from your desk. Go for a walk in the woods, find a quiet place and read a book, explore something new in your neighborhood...do something that resets your mind. Take yourself out of your tangle of confusion and focus on nothing else except decompressing and renewing your sense of life.

Release Your Fears

Often, we become afraid of success for one reason or another and when we become afraid, we tend to sabotage ourselves. We lose our motivation through this fear and we try to convince ourselves that things really are "okay" as they are. Rather than forcing yourself to live in such a self-limiting way, try just letting go. Release your fears, realize that they are only limiting your potential. Use your need to release fears as your driving force to success, you have to become someone new, you can't let your fears limit your success any longer!

Popular Business Approaches for Improving Motivation

In addition to utilizing apps and making modifications to our behavior and approach to things, there are also several corporate techniques that are perfect for improving motivation.

Utilize Incentives

Plenty of larger corporations utilize incentives to motivate employees to succeed. Even if you are not the owner of a large corporation, however, you can implement incentives in your own life. Encourage yourself to succeed by setting up incentives to reward your completion of certain milestones. These incentives can be as simple as taking a day of PTO to just relax or buying a new bottle of nail polish, but pick something that truly motivates you to continue focusing on success.

Recognize Achievements

Another method that corporations commonly utilize to motivate employees to continue to work hard, is to use recognition as a reward. When someone is recognized for their achievements, they feel more accomplished and more valuable for the assets that they have given. Even if you are a solo entrepreneur, you can implement recognition of achievements by sharing your achievements with friends and family!

Tradeshows, Conventions, and Extended Education

Tradeshows, conventions and extended education are all frequently used tools to improve motivation. These events all serve to connect with other individuals with similar goals as well as to promote further education in a particular area of interest. Often, these events will expose new methods of completing tasks or new advances to help to get tasks done more efficiently. These types of discoveries and advancements can serve as motivating factors for many individuals as they see just how much progress can be made when they put their mind to it.

Chapter 7 – Increasing Your Attention Span

Motivation improves focus and focus improves attention span. Just how important is it to have an increased attention span, however? Harvard University did a study on how long people's attention spans were and how focused they were on a particular job at hand. It seems that as few as 53 percent of our waking moments are focused on what we are doing. That doesn't mean just in the workplace, it refers to the time between the moment that you wake up until the moment that you go to sleep. The other 47 percent of our time is spent with our minds elsewhere. Whether this is distraction due to in interruptions, thoughts about a past event or worries about a future event, that 47 percent of our life is wasted because we are not actually concentrating on the moment we are in. 47 percent of our time is lost, wasted on non-productive tasks because we simply aren't paying attention.

Why is Attention Important?

You may be wondering to yourself, if you can conduct a task without paying attention to it, what's the big deal? Why is it so important that each task that you undertake involves your full attention span? As long as the task is finished, who cares, right? Wrong! Attention plays a crucial role in both our work lives and our personal lives. Attention is not only what helps us to learn how to do things correctly and avoid danger, but it also helps to improve ourselves and accomplish bigger and better things. Attention, paired with focus, is what makes millionaires, millionaires.

So what can you do to improve your attention span to ensure that your future is open up to success? Let's take a look.

Implement Attention Span Improvement Apps

There are a good many apps out there designed to improve and grow attention spans. These apps focus on training your attention to focusing on details and achieving success. Let's take a look at some of the most popular of these smart phone, tablet, and PC apps below.

1. Self-Control – Self-control is a free app that allows users to block websites that serve as regular distractions for a set period of time. This eliminates the temptation to visit websites that become a "time suck" and end up destroying half of your work time and all of your productivity.

2. TrackTime – A 99c app, TrackTime works by tracking every move you make on your computer, tablet, or smart phone and when prompted, it produces an audit of that time. A great way to track where your lost hours in the day are really going, TrackTime is the best method of motivating yourself to pay more attention.

3. Focus Booster – A free and premium app, Focus Booster aims to improve your focus and attention span by utilizing a Pomodoro technique of time tracking. By setting specific 25 minute slots for tasks and arranging a short 5-minute break between tasks, you are able to maintain an adequate level of

focus and concentration on each task without becoming burned out.

4. CogniFit – A free brain-training app, CogniFit not only serves to improve focus, memory, and concentration, but it also serves to exercise your brain throughout the day so that you are continually growing. Don't let your brain waste away, instead work on creative growth and improving your attention span with daily exercise.

5. Elevate – This free app was originally developed to assist those with ADD and ADHD, but over time it has also become a popular app for those with any type of concentration difficulties. This app focuses on creating a catered training program for your needs that adjusts as you continue to practice with it daily.

Skills You Can Use to Increase Your Attention Span

In addition to using apps, there are also some great alterations you can make to your life to improve your attention span. These alterations can vary from something as simple as changing a routine to something as seemingly tedious as continually challenging your limits.

Sleep!

We all know that sleep is important to proper functioning, but it is also important to optimal functioning as well. No matter who you are or what you are trying to achieve, your success hinges on getting a full night's sleep. What makes up a full night's sleep? At least 8 hours of undisturbed sleep in your bed in a quiet room, without technological interruptions! Fail to do this and you will quickly learn how much of an impact a lack of sleep can have on your ability to concentrate.

Music

Many studies have shown that listening to music that does not have lyrics – for example, classical music, can improve our ability to concentrate on something. If you find yourself having difficulty focusing, just throw on a little Mozart and see if you find yourself more able to function.

Keep Tabs on the Clock

When we suffer from a lowered attention span, we often end up wasting more time than we have to waste in the first place. Set yourself an alarm or keep tabs on the clock when you feel like you are running low on attention. If, after a set amount of time you are still not making progress, step away from the task and focus on something else or take a break. After at least 5 minutes or so, try to tackle this topic again. Just don't allow your time to be eaten up by sitting and staring at a problem and trying to will yourself to concentrate harder.

Popular Business Approaches for Improving Attention Span

In addition to the changes mentioned above, there are some

great corporate strategies used to increase the attention span in the workplace. These strategies are frequently utilized on CEO's and workers alike and have long proven successful. Let's take a look at some of the more popular of these approaches.

Take Breaks and Work Slowly!

It seems somewhat counterintuitive for any tip for success to contain the word "slowly." The truth is, however, that when faced with significant amounts of information to weed through, we quickly tend to lose focus. If instead, we work slowly and break that large amount of information down in to a few smaller pieces and read those, we maximize our short attention span while still getting the job done in a reasonable amount of time! The goal here is not to allow yourself to become overwhelmed.

Eliminate Unnecessary Distraction

Many workplaces encourage employees to eliminate unnecessary distraction from their immediate area in order to discourage distraction from the task at hand. By removing distractions, you are creating a healthier environment for your attention span.

Take Notes

Note taking is a skill that seems to have fallen by the wayside for many, but successful corporation owners know the importance of taking notes in order to cater to a low attention span. Of course, it is always better to work on growing your attention span, but while you are working on that, take notes during activities that prove challenging. Instead of trying to force yourself to pay attention throughout the whole thing, listen and take notes. These notes will not only serve as a reminder when your attention span has completely run out, but they will also provide you with a reference for later use.

Chapter 8 – The Connection Between Stress and Focus

A short attention span can be a real detriment to your ability to focus and succeed in the workplace, but so too can stress. The University of Maryland Medical Center has a great article on how stress impairs concentration and in particular, it notes that stress can cause high blood pressure which can lead to other serious ailments. The study also found that stress can interfere with sleep schedules which then damage our productivity and our ability to function normally. Simply put, stress is everything we don't want or need when it comes to striving for success.

Stress creates sleep disturbances, it causes poor attitude and inability to handle problems, it promotes an unhealthy buildup of toxins within the body, and it just simply, wears and tears on the body and mind until we find ourselves feeling helpless. So where is all of this stress coming from? The simplest answer is, the way that you live.

The way that you live your life affects your level of stress and consequently, your level of concentration. If you are constantly stressed, you won't be able to focus on work and then you won't be able to complete that work as successfully as someone who is less stressed. Thus, you need to address the stress in your life in order to bring your lifestyle back into balance. What kinds of things can you do to make this type of positive change? Let's take a look!

What Can You Do to Lower Your Stress Levels?

Exercise!

Rarely do people want to hear that exercise is the answer to their problems, but in the case of high levels of stress, exercise is the answer to the problem! Exercise not only takes us away from the stressors that are influencing our ability to function, but it also releases those incredible endorphins that make us feel as though we could accomplish anything! A daily dose of endorphins is an incredibly powerful solution to a buildup of stress in anyone's life!

Create a Support System

Oftentimes we begin to feel stressed when we are overtaxed. When we are juggling too many responsibilities with no one to help us to "take the wheel" once in a while, we can become overwhelmed and simply want to stop functioning all together. In order to avoid this from happening, build a support system around you who are able to help you in both your personal and your business life. This support system can be coworkers who don't mind helping with the odd project here and there, or the spouse who cooks dinner in order to give you a little free time. It doesn't matter who they are or what responsibility they take, relieving some of your stress will immediately improve your overall health and your ability to focus.

Eat a Healthy Diet

In the above chapters we have already touched upon the importance of a healthy diet. When we eat the right foods and provide our body with the nutrients that it needs to function properly, we also cope better with higher levels of stress! This is because the more efficiently our body's function, the more efficiently they can react to stressors. Additionally, when our bodies are functioning optimally, we are less distracted by symptoms of it malfunctioning! These symptoms can not only cause a distraction to our ability to work, but they also contribute to physical discomfort both of which lead to more stress which we are unable to regulate properly and a resulting inability to focus.

Balance Work and Life

Balancing work and life optimally is a skill that very few people have been able to master. This does not mean, however, that you should not try! A healthy balance between work and home not only means not being a workaholic, it also means knowing how to separate work life and home life. For example, if you are maintaining healthy hours at work, yet when you come home all you talk about is work, then you are not keeping a healthy balance and you are increasing the chances that you will become stressed to a point of breaking. It doesn't matter when your role is within your company, if you want to succeed and be able to focus on success, you must know how to balance your work and family life without allowing the two to overlap.

Stress Reduction Apps

If you find that you have difficulty putting some of the changes above in to action to reduce your personal stress levels, you may find a smartphone, tablet, or computer app can help you. There are a good many apps designed to help reduce stress levels so that you can better focus, a few of these are listed below.

1. Breathe2Relax – Breathe2Relax is a free and paid app that is designed to help you to focus on mindful breathing in order to reduce stress. With various breathing exercises that have been proven to reduce the bodily stress response, this app is a great way to become more skilled at releasing the stress in your life.

2. Personal Zen – A free gaming app, Personal Zen is designed to help you to train your brain in to a more positive frame of mind. A clinically proven game for reducing negativity, Personal Zen can decrease your stress for the day in as little as 25 minutes and reframe how you approach future challenges.

3. 7 Minute Workout – A free app, 7 Minute Workout focuses on the benefits of exercise in fighting back against stress. By providing a simple 7-minute workout that doesn't require a gym, this app gives you the benefit of health and lowered stress levels and no room for excuses!

4. Time Out – Yes, you read that right. A free app that offers in app purchases, time out is designed to build breaks in to the average workday to optimize focus and concentration while decreasing stress. With the ability to set up longer 10 minute breaks once an hour, or shorter 15 second breaks every 15 minutes, Time Out forces break time by dimming out the main screen for the designated period of time. These breaks allow for regular stretching as

well as serve as a reminder to step away, take a breath and look at things with a fresh face a few minutes later.

5. Plasticity – A free app, Plasticity is designed to make the workplace a more enjoyable place to be. By encouraging you to see the positive things in your work environment, this app pushes you away from stress inducing negative thinking and promotes healthier and more enjoyable workplace relationships.

Popular Corporate Tactics for Stress Reduction

Apps and behavior modification are both incredibly helpful interventions for reducing stress levels, but there are also some very effective corporate tactics for reducing stress that are worth noting as well. Let's take a look at some of the most commonly and successfully utilized.

Schedule Balancing

A particularly helpful trick that many corporate moguls utilize to keep their stress levels moderated, is schedule balancing. Schedule balancing means not only balancing work and home life, but it also means balancing activities in the workplace. Know your limits and the resources that you have to work with so that you can speak up when you feel that you are being overwhelmed. Balance your daily schedule with tasks that are distributed according to when you work best, and don't take on more than one significant project at once! By having this type of scheduling awareness, you are more able to avoid the stress of being overworked.

Mandatory Break Times

There is a reason that most corporations build mandatory break times in to employees schedules – without breaks, employees become stressed with being constantly at work and being bombarded with work related requests. It doesn't matter if you are a grocery bagger or a CEO, breaks are a necessary part of keeping stress levels low and increasing the level of focus and dedication given to the job.

Communicate!

Bosses, managers, and other figures of authority in the workplace should always encourage communication as a means of keeping stress levels low. Whether stress comes from being overscheduled, having personal issues, or having a conflict with a fellow worker, communication is the key to preventing these stressors from escalating to a point of failure. If you feel yourself beginning to become stressed as the result of someone else's actions or inactions, speak up. Communicate with that other person or, if this isn't possible, communicate with your supervisor so that you can find a resolution to the problem. The longer you allow issues to fester, the less focus you are going to have on your work, the angrier you are going to become, and the worse the outcome of your stressful situation is going to be.

Ensure that there is an Opportunity for Growth

Whether you are the owner of a company or someone who works for the company, you must always ensure that there is an opportunity for growth. Feeling trapped in a dead-end job is an incredibly common stressor for men and women in the workforce, but providing opportunity for growth, helps to prevent this. When a worker (or you) knows that there is a chance to excel and grow within the company, there is motivation to work hard and there is less stress over being trapped in a job that is going nowhere. This motivation and lowered level of stress results in more success in the workplace and increased concentration and focus.

Seek and Provide Help

Sometimes stress becomes so much that we are unable to cope with it on our own, which is precisely why many corporations these days provide mental health counseling opportunities. These services are an invaluable resource for all individuals regardless of their workplace status. If you find yourself experiencing overwhelming levels of stress, make an appointment with one of these counselors to talk it over. They may be able to provide you with other coping techniques as well as ways to reduce the stress in your life as well. If you find someone else in your workplace struggling with high stress levels, consider referring them to the workplace counselor in order to help them to cope. It doesn't really matter if it's you or your coworker dealing with overburdening stress, because eventually, everyone in close proximity is going to be impacted! So keep these medical resources in mind at all times.

Conclusion

In the chapters above, we have shared with you a number of the more commonly encountered challenges to workplace success. All of these challenges in some way reduce your ability to concentrate and truly focus on your attention on meeting the goals you set for your personal accomplishments. The good news, however, is that by utilizing the methods covered in the corresponding chapters, you can soon begin to experience a dramatic rise in your productivity. Whether you are struggling with distractions in the workplace or coping with high stress levels, all of the tips provided can help you to become healthier and more focused on your overall success.

Just remember, regardless of the job you work, only you can be held responsible for your own success. Stop blaming distraction, high stress levels, a poor attention span, and poor health habits for your failure, instead, begin to make the changes needed to succeed. Increase your focus, improve your concentration, and best of all, create a happier life of accomplishment for yourself and stop coming up with excuses. Your future is you.

I wish you the best of luck!

Dane Taylor

Want more great content? Get the expanded and updated versions of my books, available on Kindle now:

To make this bundle more easily readable, the books you read in this bundle are the 2nd Edition versions of the books.

Each individual book is available on Kindle now with more in-depth, expanded content! You'll get more detailed advice in the following editions:

Organize Your Day: 17 Easy Strategies to Manage Your Day, Improve Productivity & Overcome Procrastination

Get the 3rd Edition of this book on Amazon now:
http://www.amazon.com/Organize-Your-Day-Productivity-Procrastination-ebook/dp/B014ZQ29G2

Time Management: To-Do List Strategies to Become a Productivity Master and Get Things Done

Get the 3rd Edition of this book on Amazon now:
http://www.amazon.com/Time-Management-Strategies-Productivity-Techniques-ebook/dp/B0190D49SG

Did you like this bundle?

If you liked this book (or if you didn't), I'd love to hear your feedback and if it helped you. I welcome all feedback and use it to make my books better, so please leave a review for the book on Amazon if you have 30 seconds, you can do it here!: http://www.amazon.com/Time-Management-Productivity-Organized-Productive-ebook/dp/B01EESQKSO

Questions? Concerns? Please email us at epicpublishingbooks[at]gmail.com.

16940135R00119

Made in the USA
Middletown, DE
26 November 2018